# BIG
# DESIRE

*A Memoir*

AMY MANNINO HENRY

# CONTENTS

# ACKNOWLEDGMENTS

**My journey to this point is a winding one**, but there are people who impacted me so greatly, I feel honored God put them on my path.

To my beautiful, magical, perfectly imperfect children, Cason, Sophia, Colt and Brooklyn, who teach me lessons every day and give me unconditional love and acceptance, and have and will always be my greatest blessings of all. My desire for you is to find God's purpose by trying, failing, succeeding and learning along the way in this beautiful journey of life. Remember, you are the driver of your boat, so always dream big and bold because the possibilities of life are limitless, and you hold the key.

To my parents, whom I love with all my heart. I am deeply honored that God knew I needed strong, loving leaders to guide me through life. Their selflessness and the boundless love they show towards each other, their dogs, their children, and their grandchildren is truly beautiful to witness.

To my siblings, Tara, John, Christi, Leslie and Michael, who have been there to witness all my phases in this wild and crazy life. We all play our roles within the big Italian family, and it has made life so much more colorful when you add spouses and all the cousins to the mix. And the cousins keep coming!

To my friend Laine Walker, whom I call my "Spiritual Friend" who helped me grow in my spiritual relationship with God, in the darkest hours when I felt so lost in the chaos around me as my purpose in my next phase of life had not yet been revealed. Laine never let me hide away and was tenacious in making sure I made it through.

To my three besties, Megan Lawson, Debbie Wade and Jersey Jen (Jennifer Griffin), who love me so unconditionally and are my sounding board and confidants, throughout this wild ride, even though at times, it played out like "Days of Our Lives" soap opera. Their daily advice (sometimes two to three times a day) and unending caring and compassion got me through all the uncertainty life threw at me and still keep me going. We are Soul Sisters forever.

To Roman Fortin, owner of The Forum Athletic Club in Atlanta, who pivoted my life journey seventeen years ago and for which I am forever grateful. I would never have started down the wellness path without your encouragement and guidance. He not only was instrumental from a coaching perspective, but he also guided me towards the nutrition and wellness path as a career. And I stand by this fact: Fast Twitch is THE best strength training class in the world and definitely in Atlanta.

To Krishna Cheruvu, who had the insight and the universe working through him, to reach me, when I was unable to find the answers externally. He guided me towards meditation and yoga and helped me find answers by turning inside and listening to my inner voice, which is God. He taught me what synchronicity is and towards the concept that "there are no coincidences in life". I am a believer in this concept 100% now.

To Candi Cross, my editor, who instantly understood my vision. She grasped my story, embraced my quirky writing style, and saw the potential of The Desire Empire I had envisioned. With keen insight, she crafted a plan to introduce my Desire Method to the world.

To Beth Oden, my creative website designer, whose expertise goes far beyond her impressive technological skills and extensive experience. Through synchronicity, I found her after praying for guidance. Beth has become a mentor and guide as I developed my online 28-Day Desire Method Transformational Wellness program to benefit those who feel stuck. Our collaboration is extraordinary, resulting in a beautiful digital presence. I invite you to explore the fruits of our labor at *www.thedesiremethod.com.*

Finally, to the Catalyst, an individual who helped open my eyes to my true path, igniting my inner spark of courage I needed to be unapologetically and authentically me. Epically grateful.

These individuals had a major impact on my life, and I am forever thankful for them. My hope for you, my dear reader, is that from my story you can open your eyes up to the possibility of self-discovery and purpose.

I want to be your Catalyst. All it takes is one voice, one thought, one person's connection with you, or even a random chance meeting (synchronicity at work) to change the direction of your life, guiding you towards your desired life. Remember, you are not stuck. You do not have to settle. You do not have to feel your age or give up on the things that make you feel most alive. We all hold the power within to create a beautiful, epic life and it starts with opening your eyes to the limitless possibilities and surrounding yourself with those who lift you up and help to illuminate your path.

# Introduction

# DANCE OF DESIRE

"Dreams come true when desire transforms into concrete actions."

—*Napoleon Hill*

**Ballet was my heart and soul.** I desired to dance all day long. The graceful movement, the fluidity, the music, the costumes, the lights. I was a star, after all. I was made to be on a stage, and ballet was the vehicle for which all my dreams would come true.

In the fourth grade, I nailed "Flashdance" for the talent show, basking in the glory of every movement and the fanfare from my audience under the lights. *What a feeling.* Neighbors still come up to my mother and talk about my performance that day. How I turned our Catholic elementary school into a house of dreams for a few minutes. I danced with abandon, but in the back of my mind, I knew I did not fit the mold.

Ballerinas can't be big. So, my dream was stomped on for many years after as I tried my hardest to mold into a lithe, small-boned person. Obviously, that was impossible, so I blamed myself. I blamed my body. My body held me back. My size, my bigness.

I buried this resentment, this hatred for myself deep down. But that self-disgust was in there. It was in a weed. Planted and protected within my subconscious, weaving a web, a spider web throughout my subconscious mind. I wasn't good enough. I was too big. I wasn't worthy of having such a lofty dream. How dare I think I could be a ballerina. Who did I think I was?

We spend our lives resenting the parts of us that held us back from the dream we had as children, and that resentment manifests within our consciousness as self-loathing. A child's first blush of self-love is attached to something the world has, that we want to be. It becomes our identity, it defines us because there are no limits or roadblocks when we are kids, and our imagination can take us anywhere and visualize us as anything, even flying in the clouds or landing on the moon!

You define yourself as something, which becomes a child's inaugural version of identity and love. "Truck driver!" "Pilot!" "Fairy Princess!" We all have that spark resonating in early years. Ask anyone in the room. They know exactly what they wanted to be when they grew up. And then society or tainted years of experience reached out for the belief, that dream, with the oversized hands of a gigantic monster and forbade us from living it. We resented whatever part of our body that wasn't good enough to fulfill our dreams. Your mind? Not smart enough to be a doctor. Your height? Not tall enough to be a famous basketball player. Or maybe your body was like mine. I couldn't *really* think that I could be a ballerina, dancing with the New York City Ballet or kicking in the line as a Rockette.

My body betrayed me. The size of my body was the roadblock in front of my dreams. If only I were smaller, shorter, more sinewy. Now, obviously this trauma to my soul didn't happen overnight but started as a black hole, a rip in the fabric of my subconscious, innocent mind, that slowly began to grow larger as I navigated life with the burden of a big body.

I spent my whole life hating my body, damaging it. Diets on and off, extreme calorie restriction, binge eating, exercise anorexia. I was not aware of what was driving my beliefs and behaviors because it was the darkness within my subconscious mind that stored all those negative memories, emotions and thoughts about my big body. My identity became my body. And so, I reflected that negative image of self-hatred onto the world. I had a ton of friends, but that ugly inner voice would always have me notice how small they were, how lithe they were, how dainty their feet were, the picture of femininity.

I thought everyone was saying to themselves, "Oh, she's a big girl." In reality, no one's noticing anyone else. They're worried about themselves and dealing with *their* subconscious beliefs they also carry within themselves. Many of us are walking around projecting our beliefs about ourselves on others with no awareness.

You see, my whole life I was described physically as "the big girl" with big arms, big shoulders, big boobs. I am tall, standing at 5'10" and because society values the daintiness of women, my physical features were always being called out. It was like society didn't really know what to do with me—I was pretty and tall and big boned, with big eyes, a big smile and a big personality. I would walk in a room and heads turned to the "exotic" animal who just appeared. Now, don't get me wrong, I was born with the love of performing, but that inner spark within me, the essence of me, got dimmed quickly by society. The seeds of self-doubt, self-worth, sense of self, got buried deep within me as society planted its weeds. Those weeds grew over my self-concept, telling me that I was different, an outlier, not the norm—in a land where the average height of a woman was 5'2", who weighs 120 pounds.

My resentment was so intense that my belief was that the only thing people saw was my bigness. I projected my disdain of my body onto others. So, the reflection was that people notice my size first, and my personality second. My subconscious mind stored this trauma.

There's a time capsule of childhood trauma in every one of us and it's buried deep. Yet it impacts and manifests itself throughout adult life through our thoughts, feelings, and behaviors. Each of us has answers we spend our lives seeking. And the purpose of life equates to bringing those answers up to the surface, the conscious, to shine light on them in order to heal and evolve as authentic beings. Our journey in this life is about finding our authentic selves.

Within the subconscious, all answers lie within us waiting to be dug up and released like a dove hidden in a cage under a blanket. Our authentic self is waiting to be taken out of the darkness. The cage door opens, and the authentic self can fly free. Freedom is what we seek. Freedom to be who God has intended.

I will no longer be hidden in the dark shadows, playing small. Never again, *Never again.*

The thing about desire is that it never goes away. It's glowing within whether you choose to act on it or not. The day or long night you allow it to engulf you over all the negative, repressive, foreign matter you've poured in to pollute it—and pollute YOU—*that* desire will turn into manifestation.

I had to walk this journey, lose myself to big beliefs, opinions and judgments of the external world, only to fiercely and courageously break free from my self-imposed box I was living

in, in order to inform others. There is another way, a bigger way to live life on your terms, based on your inner fire. Your desired life.

*—Amy Mannino Henry*

# Chapter 1

# SEED OF SELF-LOATHING

"Imagination is the beginning of creation. You imagine what you desire, you will what you imagine, and at last, you create what you will."

—*George Bernard Shaw*

**Think about when a little kid makes eye contact with you.** They dial in, almost wanting to have a staring contest with you. You realize they are peering into your soul, trying to connect to the smaller version of you in there, the one that's playful and full of joy and dreams. They seek to see the glimmer of that little kid and just like that, you start to smile, and make funny faces at them. Children bring out the inner child within us and for a moment, we allow our guard down for the child to come out to play.

Children are in wonder of their world, whether it's water running downhill in the gutter, seeing how a rock creates ripples in a pond, or even what your hair feels like to touch.

Children are so immersive about connecting and learning. More importantly, they're experts in using their imagination. We spend a small amount of our time being unaware of societal norms and structure and that's when a child acts goofy, throws herself on the floor in a tantrum, screams, belly laughs, does funny movements with her face—as a child, you think you literally hung the moon because you exist. That's it. You are just being and that is a gift to the world and you, at that time, believe it. Each of us are told we could be anything we wanted. There are no limitations. Use your imagination.

I used my imagination in a big way. I spent my time pirouetting around the house, leaping, not walking, jumping up with my toes pointed with precision because I lived and breathed ballet. I refused to wear pants and instead, always a tutu or frilly dress for flair. That was my heart and soul. I owned it. I lived it.

I always knew I was a star destined for a life filled with tulle, tights and toe shoes. Think about it—whether we like it or not, we all are the main "star" of our lives, even if we haven't learned to embrace it yet. Ever since I was a little girl growing up on an acre of land in Little Washington, Pennsylvania, I had big dreams and in synchronistic fashion, my favorite cat as a child was aptly named "Star".

I was a ballerina. To me, ballet was pure love and freedom. Pure joy. I loved everything about movement merging with music, a visual plethora of glitter, power and grace. I loved the feeling of being light and unshackled, free to leap, spin, and twirl everywhere. My vision was to become a Rockette and dance in New York City. Oh, and the dream didn't stop at just dancing. The performance bug bit me and never let go.

I have a clear memory, around the age of three where I fell into limerence with dance. Picture a large room, surrounded with mirrors, metal chairs lining the front so all the parents could watch their little girl go through positions and pirouettes. The moms all sitting cross legged and aware—no cell phones to distract or capture the moment with. Me, I was too excited to stay seated on my mom's lap, watching my older sister, whom I will introduce you to in a bit, so I was standing just a tad in front of the parents.

I became so focused and mesmerized by the ambiance of the music merging with the graceful poses, that I slowly began to back up without turning around to see where I was going. I found a lap I deemed was my mother's, and proceeded to cozy myself up to her, again without taking my eyes off the dancing. Something in me must have felt off; we are all energy, after all, and I might have sensed a different energy or smell. I turned back and up and was eye to eye with a total stranger, who had a big grin on her face. Panicking, I swiveled my head around desperate to find my safe space in the arms of my mom, when I saw she was three seats away laughing kindly with the stranger whose lap I had been occupying for a couple minutes. I remember being very unsettled and freaked out after, not understanding at the time how blind one can become to the world when passion enters.

My favorite birthday present arrived when I was in preschool: a sparkly red tutu. I'll never forget it and wore it every day for over two months, to the point where it became frayed. This was way before you could walk straight into Target and get any sparkly dress imaginable, so that tutu was rare and hard to replace. I pirouetting around the house, leaping, not walking, jumping up with my toes pointed just so the red sparkles glittered in the window light. I lived and breathed ballet. My dreams were big, my costumes were big, and my personality was big. But my world redefined the word, *big*, for me to a negative term. Before that, I had not thought about my body being big or the space it occupied. It was fluid, carrying me through my little world and often to music. Such a lyrical, little life! Comparing my body to other kids' bodies was not on my radar. Why would it be? I was only five.

That year, one man changed the course of my life forever. That fucking man—a doctor, no less. This doctor, whose name I have forgotten and so will call him "Dr. X" (I visualize him as Dr. Evil from Austin Powers, actually), changed my life so completely with his judgment of my future self that it took me decades to take my power back from him. I have no idea if he's alive or dead now, but he impacted my life in such an extreme manner that I can't tell my story without him. His opinion shaped just about every thought, action, and belief I had about myself from that point forward and started my hatred toward the word, *big*.

Dr. X fucked me up more than any other person—or rather, I allowed the "story" Dr. X told to fuck me up. You might be thinking, damn, this Dr. X must have done something horrific, right? Not exactly. He didn't beat me or abuse me physically, thank goodness. Instead, he planted a seed in my head that allowed the vines of self-loathing and insecurity to grow within me. Unknowingly, I gave him power over how my life would play out, and he probably has no recollection of ever meeting me, which is the pitiful part.

The story goes that my mom took my older sister, Tara, and I to the doctor for our wellness checkups. My big sister was tall and lean. She was the one who had the ballerina body, the only type of body dance studios revered at the time. I was shorter, more muscular, and broad shouldered with a bit of a belly. I was, by no means, overweight or "thick", just built completely differently than her. Yet, Dr. X scanned me and then her, and you know what he told my thin, tall, stunning mother?

He said, "You had better watch this one. She's going to be chunky, and that will lead to sugar diabetes and heart problems later in life."

It wasn't solely a comment about my weight. It was a judgment on my dreams, my worth, my very being. It planted a seed of doubt so deep, it would take root and grow into a forest of self-doubt and body hatred. In my young mind, being "chunky" meant I couldn't be a ballerina. If I couldn't be a ballerina, who was I? What was I worth? My subconscious, ever vigilant and protective, absorbed this message. It began to see my body not as the instrument of my passion, but as the enemy, the big thing standing between me and my dreams.

Simultaneously, that scary comment, expressed by an authoritative figure to my loving, young mother, changed my life forever. The image Dr. X painted for my mom of an overweight,

unhealthy, disease-ridden daughter sent her into a pure panic—
and damn, no wonder.

Some background on my mom: She is a force to be reckoned
with—a brilliant multi-tasker, ball-busting, get-the-job-done
kind of woman. A nurturer by nature, my mom is an extreme
lover of animals and children, having given birth to six children
and cared for multiple dogs, cats, and birds. She possesses a level
of selflessness I have rarely encountered in my life. There's a
problem, and by goodness, Teri will take action to fix it with speed
and efficiency. Her mottos are "I'll handle it" and "Don't worry
about it; I'll make it work". She is, by definition, "action oriented".

So, based on my mom's personality, that brief encounter with
the motherfucking doctor caused her to do the best she could
to process the information and create an action plan. Another
Teri motto is, "I am only as happy as my least happy child."
Suddenly, she envisioned me as overweight, living alone, sick,
and uncomfortable as an adult after Dr. X painted a bleak picture
of what he saw. She didn't want that life for me. Who wants their
child to be sad, lonely, and unhealthy? So, I do not blame my
mom for what followed. She was and is the most incredible mom
on the planet *(#truth)*.

Out of fear, Mom put me on a diet. Yes, a five-year-old.
You might be thinking to yourself, *big deal*, because the level of
overweight and obese children has skyrocketed in the last forty
years. Back in the 80s, though, it was practically unheard of.
Let's be clear: I was not overweight, obese, or even chunky. Dr.
X implanted the fear of God in my mom that I *might* become
chunky, *might* develop diabetes, *might* have heart issues in the
future. Do you see why I think of him as Dr. Evil?

Thus, the five-year-old Amy, who dreamed of stardom on the
stage of life, became aware that the outside world saw her as "big".
Notice I said the "outside world". I didn't think I was big, but now

that Dr. X deemed it, my little mind began to change the way I saw myself, in the eyes of others. I crashed down to Earth with a thud, feeling my bigness, feeling my body, and feeling shame. It didn't stop me from continuing to wear my sparkly red tutu or change how I acted as a ballerina, per se, but it made me hyper-aware of my body size compared to other kids, which is not normal or healthy in the least.

I have vivid memories after that visit of sitting on the floor in kindergarten, the colorful rug with a large circle of letters and numbers making a big ring. Each of us sat on a number or letter during snack time and as I watched the other kids opening the Twinkie and Ho Hos packages, Oreos and potato chips, there sat little "big" Amy, opening her snack bag filled with carrots and celery. That was the moment I knew I was different. In the mind of little Amy, I didn't deserve the sweet treats the other kids got because I was big. That was the moment I looked at sweets in a whole new light and put them on a shiny pedestal for some time to come.

Even after all these years, I am still a ballerina because my biggest joy in life is dancing to music; it is my flow state, where mind, body and spirit are in synergistic alignment. Regardless of Dr. X's comment, I continued taking ballet lessons to begin my journey to New York City, to be a Rockette. Dance is like gymnastics, though, and height and body type matter. Remember Mary Lou, the Olympic gymnast? Before she came on the scene, gymnasts were usually petite and lean. Mary Lou took the stage in the Olympics, looking like a compact bodybuilder compared to the Ukraine gymnasts. At the time, her body type wasn't the norm, yet she won the hearts of the world as she kicked ass with power and determination. She broke the body mold for girls in that sport, which remains today.In the dancing world, female ballerinas tend to be petite, lean, and of moderate height so the male dancer can easily lift her over his head. My vision of femininity was that of the principal ballerina. Here is what is interesting though: Looking at the body type of a dancer objectively now, the females seldom had any curves, no boobs or butt, shoulder bones jutting out, legs that do not touch at the thighs. My obsession with Barbie probably didn't help either. I was taller and more muscular than just about everyone at the dance studio, yet that did not prevent me from trying out for Junior Company around the age of nine because when it came to performing, my confidence was through the roof.

To make Junior Company, you needed to be good at both ballet and jazz, which I was, yet I didn't make it the first year because I showed up with my hair down and wore a purple leotard and leg warmers in true "Amy flair"! Not one to pay attention to detail (the story of my life), in my excitement at the possibility of being in the Company, I didn't notice the instructions that stated dancers must come with hair in a bun, black leotard and pink tights. Going rogue did not impress the powers that be, and with my flair taking center stage, rather than my talent, I was told I did not earn a spot that year. However, rather than give up, my internal will to keep my crazy dream alive, in spite of my bigness, gave me the push I needed to continue improving my craft and evolve as a ballet and jazz dancer.

After I tried out the following year, conforming to bun, black leotard and pink tights, I remember sprinting down the driveway as the postman slid the mail into our mailbox, opening the letter with excitement, knowing I had made it by the thickness of the envelope, a dead giveaway to being chosen. I made Company, and despite my bigness, my dreams might still have a chance to come true—here I come New York! Thus, began my four-day-a-week dance training with the Junior Company. On Wednesdays, right before we began actively stretching, we would all walk upstairs to the larger dance studio. At the front of the room, next to the stereo, the owner/former ballerina, whom I will call "Tonya", would sit in a metal chair with her hair in a bun, her legs crossed, and her character shoes pointed ("feet always pointed").

A menacing scale accompanied her. To my chagrin, part of being in the Company meant staying at the "right" weight, so it was required that each ballerina be weighed weekly. Guess who always weighed in as the heavyweight? Not an award a young girl wants.

My heart would start beating rapidly, hoping a miracle would occur and I would have dropped ten pounds from the previous week. Fear would grip me, sweat would bead on my forehead, and I would wait as she called out each name, in alphabetical order of last names. "Mannino" was smack-dab in the middle, so I would watch the dainty, indifferent nine-year-olds walk up to the scale, get on, and jump right off as Tonya yelled out each one's weight. It had literally no effect on these girls. No one was telling Tiny Dancer (the name I gave the small dancers out there) she was "big" or that she should weigh a certain amount. In my mind, she won the lottery—she would have an easy life! Tiny might not be the greatest dancer, but at least she was small and lithe and would be placed front row.

As Tonya yelled my name, I would race up, not making eye contact with the larger-than-life studio owner, step on the scale, hold my breath, try and lift my heels up so that, somehow, the scale wouldn't register my full weight, and then jump off as she called out the number. Sometimes, I jumped on and off so quickly that she would instruct me to get back on because she didn't catch my weight. Imagine how red my face got because that only prolonged my agony.

Again, note that I was well-proportioned and toned, with no fat rolls, no chunkiness anywhere. I was, and still am, swaybacked, so I tended to stand with my stomach out because my lower back was more of a "C" shape than straight. Other than that, I looked normal. But I was constantly told to "suck in" my stomach. Gee, I wonder why I developed a hatred toward my stomach. Dr. X's comments first, then getting weighed publicly a few years later, equated to what I would now consider body shaming a child. Thus, my perception of the world's opinion was that what mattered, above all, was my size—which wasn't standard. The world's opinion was noted by me, internalized, and reluctantly embraced. Dr. X planted the detrimental seed to be further fed by my ballet experience.

Girls who were far less talented than me scored better roles and placed in the front row because they were short, lithe and tiny. Trust me, I was not delusional or unrealistic in my talent. I knew I was talented and could map music and choreography in my head, yet I knew I wasn't as incredible as the lead ballerina, Christina, who happened to be the daughter of the studio owners. Groomed for the stage from when she was a wee little girl, Christina was a beautiful, talented performer. She fit all the molds—blond, average height, beautiful lines, passion. I looked up to her (not literally, of course) because she was the epitome of talent. But the other girls? I could dance circles around some of them, so even if I was in the back row (probably having more to do with my height than my weight, but as a child, I created the story that it was because I was big), I was still full of joyful freedom every time we performed.

This was the year I had my first spiritual experience and in true form, it happened while I was on stage. Always hidden in the back row due to being taller than all the other girls when suddenly everyone else, the audience, my fellow ballerinas, all seemed to fade away. The stage lights morphed into a single, warm radiant beam, shining solely on me. It was just me, basking in the bright blanket of light. I was overtaken by peace, joy, and a sense of delight as I danced with all my being. God was there. I was dancing for God and God alone. And He was acknowledging my presence, my being, telling me, "Amy, I see you, you are loved unconditionally."

That extraordinary experience is etched into my heart, forever. How long it lasted, I have no idea—maybe several minutes. But the image in my mind, the vision of this experience, is of me, looking at the back of me, a silhouette against the light of the beam, dancing and leaping and making big movements under the warmth of God's presence. I still find such beauty in silhouettes, as it is how I saw this life-changing moment.

Besides dancing, God did grant me a couple other talents. I have no talent in singing and can't play a musical instrument, but people, this chick was an athlete. My natural grace and coordination made sports effortless, much like dance. I had natural talent in swimming (butterfly was a favorite, I mean my shoulder width was good for something right?). Interesting that as an adult, I see dancing as athletic where the whole body moves as one. My confidence from dance helped me take on sports like basketball and volleyball, like a duck takes to water. With ease. The pool and the court became my stage, the spotlight less dim but there nonetheless. Around the time my athletic career blossomed, I started hitting puberty, so not only was I growing up, but also, my breasts started growing out like no one's business. I had a beautiful shape, voluptuous, but I didn't see it, as my vision was clouded by Dr. X and the dancing scale.

Not only was I "shapely", but I was also super aware of my size because I was usually one of the tallest girls in the class, reaching 5'8" by seventh grade and 5'10" in high school (taller than most boys). To top it all off, my DD chest made me stick out even more.

My legs were strong and shapely. I sported a small waist and broad shoulders. Yes, the word, "big", was the bane of my existence, so I picked up a body part to toss in the same category, the "I hate my..." body part. Many women have it—that one section they would cut off if possible because it doesn't fit the mold society deemed acceptable and feminine. Mine was my stomach.

My family genetically had a little pooch under the belly button. When I say I hated my stomach, I mean it. The shape of my body didn't matter because my damn stomach was all I could focus on. I developed a tic in which I would smooth my stomach with my left hand, and still, to this day, I catch myself doing this as an unconscious reminder to "suck it in".

When I was younger, I wanted to remind myself to hold my stomach in because I thought people cared what my stomach looked like and it didn't help that growing up Italian, with a house full of kids running around, that the staple on the table was white, refined, boxed pasta. Italians are known to be passionate and family oriented, yelling and emotional outbursts taking on center stage in life. They are also known to equate food with family gatherings and the culture dictates you should always have pasta and soup available in case guests or family pop in.

Dinners in my family always involved large portions, as both my parents cooked well, but that didn't mean food was plentiful. Can you imagine trying to feed six kids, while paying for private school and living in a nice area? Talk about financial stress. It was hard to keep enough food in the house for six growing athletes. My dad, with his Midwestern hustle values, worked two jobs for a while just to make sure my mom was able to manage the household.

Picture eight Manninos, going into Kroger after Sunday Mass, ages all over the map, voices louder than a rock concert, dual-wielding shopping carts like pros. We hit that store like a hurricane, and my little brother, John? He was the eye of the storm, wreaking havoc left and right. We each got to choose one junk food package. Whether it was sugar cereal, cookies, or chips, you got to pick. We were not the family with the pantry stock filled with every junk food available, far from it. My mom was always health conscious but knew to be a little yielding when it came to treats. And in our house, sharing wasn't just encouraged; it was the law so if you wanted something untouched? Better make sure you get home and hide that shit.

Twenty minutes of checkout hell later (the poor cashier), we drove home with visions of junk food available for days! ...Or so we thought. By Tuesday, the good stuff was gone, as the pantry started to only show spaghetti boxes and cardboard-flavored bran cereal. Thursday, it became pretty evident that the only quick food available to munch on was the leftover meatballs, apples and bananas. Cue the countdown to Sunday.

Dinner time was like a combat zone. Forks darting across the table, snagging bites from every plate. Hell, we laugh that my baby brother, Michael, never had to have his own plate because he moved from lap to lap getting his fill. To this day, he doesn't like people eating off his plate (makes sense because he never had to share like the rest of us). Me? I was busy playing mind games with myself, sneaking bites before dinner, under-filling my plate like a good, little dieter and silently planning how to sneak back into the kitchen before bed and escape the "kitchen is closed!" lecture. Talk about a recipe for food issues. Feast or famine? You bet your ass.

Pasta caused such internal conflict within me because always being on a diet, have you ever honesty measured out a half-cup of noodles? No? Don't do it. It will ruin your image of "Lady and the Tramp" enjoying a massive bowl of spaghetti and meatballs under the moon. A tiny bit of pasta on a plate is just plain depressing. I would find ways to sneak long-string bites of noodles before dinner, making sure no one saw me eating before the actual meal. At the time and for years after, I pretended that all those bites, all the snacking, didn't count as long as no one saw me. I became very adept with my first eating disorder, which I will call sneak eating or closet eating.

I coined this term as an adult to describe my vision of dieting and sneaking when I was young. *Eating in the dark, while pretending to be perfect in the light.* That was my motto. Eating was not a pleasant memory for me because I had to perform in this respect and show the world that Amy was a good, obedient, little girl. I thought I was performing for others, yet, I was actually putting on a show for myself, the truth being too painful to reconcile in my mind as a child.

Though I was still dancing and dieting into eighth grade, I was forced to choose between playing basketball for high school or sticking with dancing. My coach, Miss Adams (or "Coach A"), laughed when I said I might miss practice for required dance class. Adams loved me, saw huge potential in me with my natural athleticism and size, and knew if she could get me to focus on basketball, I could be an amazing player for her. Coach A took on a mentoring role and sat me down to explain the situation. She said, "Amy, if I let you leave practice early to go to dance class, how can I justify playing you when the other girls are fully committed?" She went on to say that I was one of only two eighth graders worthy to be pulled up to junior varsity and that was a huge accomplishment. But she warned that if I didn't commit, she would not be able to play me.

Because I was fully immersed in high school and playing an intense social game, I began to understand that leaving campus every day after school to go to dance would hinder my social life. So, I listened to what she had to say. Also, the school I went to was a bit of an anomaly because female athletes were more revered than the cheerleaders, so my ego correlating to social status won out. I wanted the glory of starting on JV as an eighth grader. I wanted my fellow classmates to be at the games, cheering me on. I would turn my passion away from the stage and become a star on the court, so I made the decision to leave my dream of dancing in New York behind.

# Chapter 2

# SCALING MY COLLEGE YEARS



**My whole life, I had labeled myself as a ballerina who played sports**—a ballerina who went to school, who had friends, who was one of six kids. But dancing also made me feel large, uncomfortable in my skin, and took me away from my social life at school. With sports, my size and talent were celebrated, and so at the age of thirteen, I gave up dancing (and my dream of being a Rockette, as I was too tall for their standards by that point). Thus, my identity had to shift from being a ballerina who played sports to being a basketball player and volleyball player. I took on the new, shiny label as it seemed much more aligned with my body type than dancer, making it much easier to wear.

I took on sports and started to create a persona as a star athlete, but you know what? It was like coming in second, the dreaded red ribbon. Not good enough for the blue ribbon, settling for second place. That was what I thought about swimming, basketball and volleyball. Although I was extremely athletic, I did not work as hard at it as I did with dance. I never dreamed of playing in the Olympics or even playing at the college level.

My journey of self-awareness, self-loathing, body dysmorphia, and eating disorders continued to morph because of the stresses of high school. Being fit and lean, I weighed less than I do now.

Did I see myself in that light? Hell no—I would have pretzels and diet coke for lunch, then go to a rigorous volleyball or basketball practice on little to no actual food. I remember sitting at lunch with friends when one of them mentioned the way she stayed thin was to chew the food, then spit it out, so at least she got the taste. I tried it, but that wasn't a diet—that was an eating disorder and lasted in my life for about two days until it became kind of unrealistic and gross to spit out food.

My big 'ole boobs were an advantage in high school, but I would still have to wear two sports bras to keep those suckers in. The football boys would come watch our practices just to see me and my other busty friend, Jill, run. They called us the Booboska Twins. So, big breasts were a positive, but big anywhere else was certainly not (the Kardashians hadn't hit the scene yet).

I always worked out, but food was the issue because of the extreme baggage associated with deprivation (care of Dr. X). You must eat every day, so I couldn't escape the issue. In college, freshman year, I became a vegetarian and decided to go on a no-fat diet, yet would continue to sneak/closet eat when my roommates were at class. Out in the light, I would eat bagels, pasta, sweets, and drink beer, but no fat. If you follow the logic of the time, that meant I would not gain fat. But the reverse happened. I gained fifteen pounds that year and became even more aware of my bigness. I should have been wearing a label on my chest saying, "I am big, but I am a dieting machine" because that is what I projected to the world. I didn't focus on the parts of me that were kind, sweet, friendly, and fun. I defined myself as big, and the scale was my God.

College was brutal, with the stress of being at an incredibly challenging academic school and trying to connect with people I thought were smarter than me, with majors like chemical engineering and electrical engineering as the norm. I don't recall ever just having a chill day that first year. You know, the day of skipping class on a beautiful Wednesday, lying in the grass on the quad, and staring up at the blue sky while pondering life? Never have I ever. Georgia Tech wasn't like some northern Ivy League school with stately brick buildings surrounded by trees and grass. Tech was in the middle of downtown Atlanta, so there was no peacefulness on campus. Even if I had attended one of those schools with a true "college" campus, I wouldn't have noticed because I was too busy trying to hide my stomach and planning my workouts.

Throughout college and after, I never shared with anyone that I was both closet eating or sneak eating, and binge eating. To the world, I was the perfect eater, a big girl who exercised and ate salads with dressing on the side. I thought I had fooled them, because hell, I had convinced my mind that the calories don't count if no one saw you consume them.

After college, when I would come home from work early (I was in sales and after going over quota each day, I could leave at 3:00 p.m.), the house would be quiet and empty, my sister and roommate still at work. I would grab a box of cereal and finish it (low fat!), I would eat sleeves of Snackwell low-fat cookies, low-fat ice cream, you name it, I would consume it (alone). And still never being able to fill the void of self-loathing with elicit food, I never felt stuffed or full. That void had been growing since I was five so unless it was uncovered and brought up to the light, no amount of low-fat anything was going to satisfy me.

I would then pretend like I was hungry at dinner and sit down with my sister and roommates and eat a full meal, thinking I had fooled everyone! But I couldn't fool my own body, and I wasn't fooling anyone. I was putting on quite a performance though, you have to admit.

With my 9:00-to-3:00 p.m. job, I pretended to be fine, making a ton of money after being poor, putting myself through college, with a boyfriend who loved me, a fun social life and great family unit. However, I allowed my bigness to control me. The scale dictated my day throughout my early twenties. I would weigh myself multiple times daily, always making excuses if the scale rose—"I'm on my period", "I ate salty food", being in complete denial that consuming thousands of extra calories of sugar-filled, low-fat, processed foods on the sly, was actually the reason the scale crept up and up.At the age of twenty-four, I got engaged to Steven, whom I dated since I was nineteen. I was at my heaviest, a size 16 and 196 pounds, having continued the "no-fat" vegetarian eating program. How do I remember my size at the very moment I was supposed to be ecstatic about such a momentous occasion? Because my body size and weight steered my happiness. My weight was always there as ball and chain, enslaving my existence and clouding my inner peace and happiness.

As I said earlier, my life was spent eating in the darkness, pretending to be perfect in the light so really, no amount of weight loss could heal the wound in my Soul; it was deep and buried within my subconscious. No diet could silence the voice of self-hatred that had taken root in my subconscious mind that dictated how I felt about myself. The more I tried to "fix" myself, the more broken I felt. Pieces with sharp edges that pricked and stabbed. When the bleeding wouldn't stop, I separated myself from my body, viewing it as a never-ending challenge to be conquered, controlled, perfected.

This journey of self-loathing and constant self-improvement wasn't only emotionally exhausting. It also led to self-isolation at times, since I thought others, too, only saw my size, not me in my entirety. As if everyone I encountered shared my debilitating obsession. Not my big smile or my big laugh, but my physical size (which again, wasn't even that big in reality).

# Chapter 3

# FACING THE CAKE

---

*"Desire is the key to motivation, but it's determination and commitment to an unrelenting pursuit of your goal—a commitment to excellence—that will enable you to attain the success you seek."*

—*Mario Andretti*

---

**When I got engaged, I decided that I wanted to be a size 12** for the wedding and lose 25 pounds, so I joined the Quick Weight Loss Center. I proceeded to torture myself for the next four months before said wedding, when a bride should be focused on smelling the rose bouquets and delighting over every detail of this rapturous life event everyone dreams of. Nope, not me. I was focused on my body size and making said body less big for my big day.

I can even remember being extremely stressed because we were supposed to go to the bakery to sample cakes for the wedding. I remember the exact layout of the bakery, the smells, the metal seats, the round white table. The image of that day is burned into my brain not because of my excitement but because I was going to have to taste cake and that was not on the Quick Weight Loss Plan. The heated anticipation caused such internal stress that I developed a stomachache.

The baker brought out three types of cakes, and because sweets are my end-all, my eyes grew large. It was like I was staring down at the most titillating, sinful thing in the whole wide world. I hesitated to pick up the fork as my mind began racing. I was torn between the vision of me, thin, in my wedding dress, and me as a five-year-old desiring the Oreos like everyone else.

Talk about a head case. I mean, it was just three pieces of cake, but the portion ballooned into the largest wedding cake from a bridal showcase because of my beliefs. I convinced myself I had to try these cakes and that all my starvation and deprivation from the past two months would not be undone with a few bites of cake, right? *Right?*

I wondered if the scale would jump 10 pounds because I ingested 500 calories of cake. That was how neurotic my mind was at the time—I was told a five-calorie piece of gum had to be included in the calorie count. Yet, here I was, sitting down to taste samples of wedding cakes for my dream wedding dreading having to wake up the next day and look down at the number on the scale, hoping it wouldn't have gone up from the day before.

Those thoughts really impacted me because although I did try the cakes and ate my fair share, I didn't enjoy the moment with my to-be husband or the cake. I was too busy shaming myself. The size of that would not permit any sweetness to enter. This happened twenty-four years ago, but I can still feel that moment. This is what we do to ourselves—we are so consumed with self-loathing and negative self-talk that we ruin moments that should be meaningful and exciting. We obliterate the precious time of our lives that we can never get back.

It didn't stop at cake, though. There were other ways I permitted the world's perceived opinion of me influence my dream wedding. I dropped down to a size 12 and felt on top of the world. I was told I was a "beautiful bride with a pretty dress" (not the Cinderella dress I envisioned as a child because, God forbid, I wear something poofy to exaggerate my size). We really had a fun wedding, which started in the afternoon at the church and lasted into the wee hours of the morning the next day. It was a party, and although the memories were amazing, the weather was perfect for an afternoon in Atlanta in August, and I was the size I wanted to be, I still remember constantly smoothing my hand over my stomach to make sure it wasn't poofy.

Going through the motions, I ate tiny bites of food and tasted both the wedding cake and the UGA Bulldog groom's cake. I had accomplished my goal weight and felt a sense of relief because I had starved myself and was miserable for four months, but I stuck to the plan and suddenly, life was good. How fragile, how fleeting.

When you set a goal like that, one that is based on a future date, some vacation or reunion, the issue is what happens *after* the event? The "why" for me was so specific, it was like I was running a marathon, and the wedding was the finish line. The sense of accomplishment was there, but what next? If the event is in the past, what is your path forward? I never thought about the day after the wedding. I was so focused on the event that it didn't matter, but there lies a major problem.

Most women flying to the Caribbean for their honeymoon to drink, eat, lay out, and have sex nonstop would probably be giddy and excited. Me? I was conflicted and stressed that I was going to allow myself to eat regular food. I could hear my five-

year-old self saying, "Be careful because what if you gain the weight back and become big again?"

Outside of my thoughts and emotions, I had unknowingly caused physical damage to my body from living off two plain chicken breasts, lettuce, and a couple of protein bars for four months. Introducing real food, rich in butter, oil, spices, and carbohydrates threw my digestive system into chaos. I was sick many times because my body did not know how to process such foods anymore. Although I wanted to enjoy the sublime, romantic dinners on the sand during sunset, I was sometimes back in the hotel room in a fetal position with horrific stomach pains.

After the honeymoon, feeling lost since my focus had been on the starvation diet for so many months, I dyed my hair from my Barbie blonde (I always said I was a Barbie Blond trapped in a brunette's body) to dark brown, moved an hour and a half away from my family where Steven was finishing law school and steadily gained back the 20 pounds.

My first year of marriage was colored by how I saw myself. It was as if I were running from myself. I hoped that if I changed the color of my hair and pretended not to notice the weight creeping back on, I would somehow not have to face the fact that I couldn't control my body weight.

My body image and self-loathing didn't impact my work ethic, though. I was raised with the traditional Midwestern values to work hard and be a go-getter. I grinded it out at work and was making a ton of money, so I couldn't understand why I did not command control over my own body. My professional success and high level of execution that always exceeded the goals only dripped drops of happiness into my being. In the back of my mind, my world revolved around the most important number I needed to see each day—my weight on the bathroom scale. I was a slave to the number, and it broke me—mentally, emotionally, and spiritually.

Then the impossible struck. My relationship with my body got even more complicated. When I was twenty-eight, I got pregnant with my first child. Though I was ecstatic at first, soon I was gripped with fear. Fear of how to mother? No. Fear that the child might have some terrible condition? No. As negative self-talk swirled in my head, I became consumed with worries about how my body would grow. What if I wouldn't be able to lose the baby weight? I would end up heavier than my husband. Fear-driven thoughts are so damaging.

However, I have to say that as my belly grew, I began giving myself a bit of reprieve. I gave myself a hall pass to enjoy being pregnant, even though I was going to get big. Due to my willpower, unlike my friends, who started eating donuts and banana splits daily because they were "eating for two", I exercised caution, meticulously consuming nourishment based on what I thought the baby needed to grow. I did not allow myself any level of food abandonment, but I did gorge on blueberries, apples and eggs—foods I knew would benefit the baby. My body responded by growing this lovely child that I carried to 41 weeks, gaining a modest 27 pounds, and my first son entered the world as a large, 9.1-pound bouncing baby, full of life and possibility.

I lost the 27 pounds, plus another five, within the year by running and pushing the jogging stroller. I know this because I tracked it in his baby book—every single week. Of course, it was always on a Tuesday, not on a Monday, because I didn't want to get on the scale after my less-strict weekend eating habits. So, I had to give myself a pass and twenty-four hours to see my true weight.

On Tuesday, I would wake up and immediately head to the scale. See, that scale would determine what I thought about myself and my body, and it was *critical* that the number I saw was lower than the week prior. If that scale showed the same number, or *gasp*, a higher number than last week, the volume of self-disgust would increase. My entire self-worth was wrapped up in an arbitrary number. That was how I viewed myself. I would shame myself, my body, my willpower. Concurrently, I would feel conflicted because I would gaze at my beautiful first-born, Cason, and realize my body had made that miracle.

This is when my deeply ingrained belief system about my body and size began to crumble slightly as light started to shine through. A little over a year later, I became pregnant with my first daughter, Sophia. Having quieted my self-loathing somewhat, being pregnant with Sophia was less traumatic because I knew I was capable of losing the baby weight. However, fear and anxiety still lingered. Fear that she wouldn't be perfect? Nope. Fear that she would have down syndrome? Nope again. My fear was that, if she was a girl, I would not be capable of raising her without having body dysmorphia or eating disorders.

I vividly remember going in for the 20-week ultrasound. I told the nurse we wanted to wait to find out the gender and asked her to write it on a piece of paper, seal it in an envelope to be opened with the family later. However, my excitement got the better of me. I recall stopping in the parking lot of the doctor's office and telling Steven I wanted to know immediately. As I opened the envelope to see the words, "It's a Girl!", written by the nurse, I burst into tears and said, "I'm going fuck this child up with my body issues!" That's how powerful a belief system can be. What should have been a joyous moment was marred by the deep-seated belief I held within me.

# Chapter 4

# SAVED BY A ROMAN WARRIOR



**My belief about my body and mentality was challenged** when I was four months postpartum from Sophia's birth. I met a trainer who would change the course of my life: Roman Fortin, a former professional football player, who owned The Forum Athletic Club in Atlanta. He believed you had to lift weights to get the muscles you wanted. As an already "big girl", I had never considered lifting weights. I was a true cardio junkie—running and spinning, that was it. Roman's influence on my belief system regarding exercise was profound and almost immediate. His method differed vastly from what the fitness industry pushed, guiding me and his other clients into a higher realm of physical fitness.

Roman Fortin was a force to be reckoned with, both physically and spiritually—a massive 6'3" human being with a welcoming smile almost as wide as his chest and arms. This former pro football player invited me for a tour of his new gym, showed me the kids' club (yes!), and began explaining his new concept, a class called Fast Twitch. He had created a circuit class designed for athletes to improve athletic performance, but valuable for anyone wanting to build muscle strength. Having just given birth, my go-to exercise was running with the jog stroller every day, so I wasn't keen on his opinion.

As he described the strength training circuit class, my eyes glazed over. I had no intention of lifting weights and was there simply to exercise and use the kids' club for babysitting during my workouts. My deep-seated belief was that I didn't need to lift weights because I was already a big chick, and no way in hell was I planning on getting "bigger". I listened politely because Roman spoke with such passion about this class! It's easy to see why people follow passion and purpose, and Roman had a solid foundation he lived by that radiated outward. He talked about different muscle fibers and the goal of each station, and I was mesmerized by his charisma and excitement. Then he paused and stared directly into my Soul, asking a question that I'll never forget—one that changed the trajectory of my life.

As I recall, Roman said, "What do you do to work out?"

My response was zealous. "I run and spin six days a week! I am a cardio queen!"

He replied, "If I were to ask you who you wanted to look like, would it be a long-distance runner?"

I said, "No, they are skin and bones and always have a pained look on their face like their knees have no cartilage left."

"What about someone who runs the Peachtree Road Race?" [The 6.2-mile race on 4th of July in Atlanta, which draws over 60,000 people annually.]

"Nah, anyone can run the Peachtree, you just have to train for it," I replied in a cavalier tone.

Then he asked, "Do you want to look like an Olympic sprinter?" Now he was going somewhere with me. I was obsessed with Madonna's cut arms since her tour in the 1990s and who could forget, what a badass Linda Hamilton looked like, rocking those guns in "Terminator 2"? Damn, that's what I wanted—definition and "cut" arms. Yes, I damn well wanted to look like a lean, strong sprinter, but how?

Roman began telling me that running and spinning for longer than 50-60 minutes forces your body to utilize muscle as fuel, so all that cardio was preventing me from getting a muscle definition. Great for the heart, he stated, just not great for muscle tone. He said if I was wanting to transform my body, I should consider backing off the long cardio sessions. He knew I loved cardio, so he recommended interval sprints on the treadmill (1 minute hard, 1 minute recovery) for up to 30 minutes max. However, to achieve the lean, muscular look, I should replace 2-3 days a week of cardio with his Fast Twitch class. Wait...what? Now, when someone tells you something that goes directly against your whole belief system, most of the time, there will be a mental pause as you teeter on the edge of an unknown abyss looking back at the familiar comfort of your normal routine.

His passion and insight and enthusiasm was infectious so I jumped off the cliff into new fitness territory and started to trust this athlete with a booming voice. I promised to try it for six months before returning to my cardio junkie routine. At the time I was about 28% body fat, nursing Sophia and holding on to about 13 pounds of fat, which is normal because your body does need fat to convert to milk, but wanted to set myself up for the lean, muscular look I appreciated and admired but deep down questioned if I was able to achieve.

This class, built for athletes, hits on every sensory level possible. Loud well-known music belting out of the speaker system with Roman breaking in to sing along every four minutes or so. Mirrors on all walls for which you could see your form and Roman pointing out if you needed to tweak the movement. The sound of metal clanking on metal as someone in the class hit a wall with their reps and dramatically released the weight, gasping for air as they bent over to rest for a couple seconds. The buzzer signals movement from one station to the next, usually giving you 75 seconds to move, put your towel down, adjust the weight and get going. There was no instruction, no downtime unless you specifically needed it or were too busy gazing at yourself in the mirror.

See, the philosophy of Fast Twitch wasn't to lift consistently for 75 seconds. The goal was to lift moderate to heavy but do it fast and hard (think like a sprinter with powerful bursts of movement) and get your heart rate up so that you "do not make the time" according to Roman. I know, this is so counterintuitive but stay with me here. Fast Twitch is designed to target your cardiovascular system by forcing your heart to go into an anaerobic state while pushing your muscles quickly to fatigue.

If you aren't familiar, "anaerobic" and "aerobic" refers to two different ways our body produces energy during physical activities. Aerobic activity can be done steadily for a sustained period of time, and your body uses oxygen to create energy. This type of exercise helps improve your cardiovascular system and endurance. On the other hand, anaerobic activities are short bursts of intense exercises where your body doesn't use oxygen as the primary source of energy. Instead, it uses stored energy in your muscles. Anaerobic exercise helps build strength, speed, and power but can't be sustained for as long as aerobic activities.

Because this class pushed my cardiovascular and strength, and was designed to build muscle, I had found my home. The ballerina, athlete, and competitor in me all emerged during Fast Twitch class. I used the beat of the disco songs to get as many reps as possible, with spot-on athletic form. I saw results quickly. My body responded to weights in a way no amount of running, spinning, or cardio ever did. By taking Roman's advice and pushing myself, I dropped from 28% body fat to 14% in eight months. I was hooked.

# Chapter 5

# METHOD OVER MADNESS

---

"Nothing great is created suddenly, any more than a bunch of grapes or a fig. If you tell me that you desire a fig, I answer you that there must be time. Let it first blossom, then bear fruit, then ripen."

—*Epictetus*

---

As I continued fine tuning my Fast Twitch game, Roman began to speak to me about spirituality and God. I grew up Catholic, going to church every week, attending Catholic school, but didn't have exposure to what differentiates religion from spirituality. I thought I had a solid relationship with God and Jesus, yet, when someone would ask me "how" I prayed, I was at a loss for words. I prayed using the prayers memorized in Catholic school—meekly and pleadingly asking God to protect me and my family—but deep down, I didn't think God cared about the little things I wanted in my life. Given my box of beliefs, obsession with my big body and subsequent habits, there hadn't been much room to discern. I assumed religion was the same as personal spirituality. In reality, they are vastly different and at times, conflicting forces. Not only was I evolving physically with strength training, but I also began to evolve in my relationship with God.

Through these ten-minute "therapy" sessions after Fast Twitch class, Roman helped me see how God directly tied to my health and wellness. He helped me to develop a personal relationship with God separate from religion. God wanted me to nurture and love the only body, the purest gift, I will ever have. God does not make mistakes, so if He made me this way, why was I trying so hard to make myself smaller and more dainty?

I had never thought of the body this way, as a unique creation of God. I only saw health and wellness as a physical construct, body parts, a formation transporting me through life, one meant to dance and jump and run, but one I was always trying run away from. I never considered the body from a spiritual side. That belief system wasn't part of the standard blueprint created for me. Roman also pointed out that our inner voice, through prayer, should be louder than external voices society wants us to listen to.

This WELLNESS awakening in the truest sense rocket fueled both purpose and insight into how my negative thoughts were hurting my spiritual relationship with God. He made me perfect, the way I was supposed to be—yet I wasn't showing love to the person He created. I realized I had to make a major change in my thoughts, feelings, and actions and protect my health and wellness in a more spiritual light, rather than just chasing the next quick-fix diet.

That year, I stopped dieting. This was a BIG step for me, as dieting had been a staple in my life for thirty years, and the grip it had on me was fierce and tight. However, I decided that for me to move forward and evolve, I had to shed the stories and beliefs that no longer served a purpose in my life, and diets had to be drowned out by new desires. I said to myself that "diet" is a bad word—a four-letter, dirty word that I will not utter to myself or speak into the universe. This decision removed my focus on keeping up with the latest diet trends and marketing ploys, allowing me to shift my energy toward more productive thoughts. Imagine not being a slave to a number on the scale all day long?

Since I had more thought space, I started uncovering an interest I never knew I had—discovering how food interacts with our bodies, down to the cellular level. I started to become fascinated by food. By nature, fascination and curiosity feel so much lighter than judgment and self-deprecation. I pursued gaining insight into what we consume every day and how it impacts everything from our energy, mood, focus, emotions, and beyond. Food is so powerful, and it needed to be understood if I truly wanted to evolve into the best version of myself. Food is medicine, food is fuel, and fuel is life.

Obviously, this focus benefited me, as I started researching and understanding how food interacts in my body, how to stabilize my blood sugar, what exercises my body responds to, what emotions are always in the background, and how my negative thoughts were preventing me from enjoying my life. I knew that if I did not address my thoughts about myself, my body, food, and exercise, I would be trapped in a negative cycle the rest of my life. I wasn't seeing the vision of myself God placed in my thoughts way back when I was five, before the world got ahold of me, but for the first time, I caught a glimpse.

However, I had a deeper drive, more than just helping myself recover from dieting, because that is what I was—a recovering dieter. The knee-jerk reaction I would get, that moment you hear about the newest magic-bullet-diet, was ingrained in me. I would read about it or hear from a friend about it and automatically begin formulating in my mind how to structure this diet in my life. All this would happen within seconds, as I was so programmed to react to the word "diet". It took mental awareness and emotional control to stop this programming and learn to talk myself into discarding any thoughts associated with trying the new diet.

Again, it took some time for my mind to stop going on autopilot, but once I was aware, I took back control, and soon, the word, *diet*, didn't elicit an emotion of hope; it elicited an emotion of disgust—exactly what I was going for! Boy, once I was able to flip the script, I felt so powerful! I wanted to give that power to other people who were struggling with the emotional attachment that the diet industry wants you to have—hope. False hope.

The diet and fitness industries want you to fail. Money keeps going to these industries when you go on and off a diet/exercise program. If you were "cured" of your bigness, these companies would have empty pockets. Thus, creating the illusion of quick-fix results gets you roped in, buying up all the supplements, books and cookbooks and such, only to realize you can't give up a whole food group or can't fit the extreme regimen into your life. I thought this was sad, and it pissed me off because I wanted others to get off the diet treadmill like I did because it creates a vicious cycle of wanting to change but not having the right tools to do so and so you continue seeking the next quick fix.

Through a connection from Roman (he impacted not only my physical and spiritual self, but guided me professionally as well), I started my own wellness company, Amy Henry Nutrition, and became a certified nutritionist and wellness speaker for corporations and groups. I craved insight and knowledge about food, exercise, sleep, supplements, and all things health and wellness related with the vision of counseling individuals and working with corporations on their wellness programs. My hope was to inspire others to find their unique wellness method, allowing them to evolve into their best selves.

My purpose, the "Why am I here?" statement became clear because I realized I had a gift. I had the gift of inspiring people to change. Those who are uncomfortable in their own skin, who feel unworthy, a sense of self hatred, who feel stuck in life and are constantly seeking answers from others to try and get the body they desire—I could actually help them change their life around!

From my years of seeing the same trend in individuals (diet hamster wheel, depression, illness, hopelessness), I created The Amy Henry Method (later, upgraded to The Desire Method) to address these disordered thoughts, behaviors and patterns. Together, my clients and I challenged the opinions they had of themselves, the self-loathing, feeling like a failure, the lack of self-love and appreciation. All these issues had to be addressed in the mind before we could permanently change the direction of their physical wellness journey.

Because I am not perfect and had life experiences (kids, job, crazy sports schedules, family obligations), I was able to connect on a deeper level with my clients. I witnessed incredible changes that started from within and radiated outward. I have been exactly where they are, and I have been through very dark times emotionally, physically and mentally. Now, I am grateful for those dark times. Darkness is where I decided to *fight* to find the light and choose to pivot my life.

In fact, my spiritual friend, Laine, helped me understand that the *Bible* passage beginning with "Though I walk through the valley of the shadow of death, I will fear no evil: for thou art with me; thy rod and thy staff they comfort me" isn't about death. She explained that it's about navigating life's trials and tribulations, recognizing we're never alone, and finding comfort in the light at the end of the dark path. Having been raised Catholic, where we didn't extensively study the *Bible*, this explanation was precisely what I needed to comprehend that we're truly never alone. God is within us and can never be separated from us.

To illustrate this concept, think of it this way: you can disown your biological father and refuse to acknowledge him, yet he remains a part of you. His DNA is within you and can never be removed. That's how God exists within us. He is an inseparable part of our being. He never promises an easy life, but He does promise simplicity when you finally discover your authentic voice and embrace your true self.

You want to know another secret? It doesn't matter what you think the world thinks about you. That is what you need to understand down to your Soul. What matters is what *you* think about yourself. What matters is there might be a dormant, little spark deep within you that needs to be ignited. Make it burn bright to reach a higher sense of self. The way you achieve this feat is by turning inward, blocking out society's ideals, and defining who and what you are at the very core of your being, which means you have to quiet your mind and remove all the noise around you for a little bit each day.

My journey of self-discovery involved peeling away layers of long-held labels, beliefs, and ideals. It was as if I were slowly removing a pair of rose-colored glasses I had worn for years. As they came off, I was startled by the vibrant hues of the world around me. The experience was akin to Dorothy awakening in the Emerald City after a lifetime in black and white—a sudden, breathtaking revelation of color and possibility that I had never before imagined.

# Chapter 6

# ACT SMALL, LOOK SMILE, AND SMILE

> "The most basic human desire is to feel like you belong.
> Fitting in is important."
>
> —*Simon Sinek*

Most will speak of their alma mater with pride, but some will try and hide their college choice. I must admit, I like telling people I went to Georgia Tech because I want them to assume I am smart, good at math, and special. Why? Because it is a hard school to get into, nationally ranked (#3 in undergrad engineering, for example, as of 2024), and people all over the world try to obtain the GT degree. Those of us who do use it to our advantage for the rest of our lives, as we should.

You know how brutal that school is? The professors were more focused on research than teaching, so most classes were taught by student assistants who weren't necessarily gifted professors. Graduates of Georgia Tech say, "I got through" rather than "I graduated". It may be a funny play on words, but it rang true—we were all drinking from a fire hose of science and technology, and to get through Tech was a special feat. Now that I am wiser about desire, I would have much preferred drinking from a keg and having fun those four years, but I digress.

On the flip side of university pride, I have a friend who didn't go to college, yet he is a successful business owner. He took a different path, a successful one, but doesn't like talking about college because he assumes people judge him over his choice to not attend one. That label is stuck to him like glue—he has given it such power throughout the years that he braces himself when the topic comes up, and he is in his forties. We give such power to labels that just becoming aware of which labels we identify with is the first step toward awakening.

Women in particular love labels of all shades and decor; the ones projected onto them by the world, those they show to the world, and the internal ones they hold. I've learned the hard way your worth should never be wrapped up in labels. To move forward (and inward), you must uncover all the labels that define you—the ones you have been using, in your mind and thoughts, to form your identity. This is not to be confused with your authentic self. Your authentic self is who you are on the Soul level before society got ahold of you. Your identity is how you present yourself to the world, and the way you present your identity is through the labels you wear.

Some women crave and buy high-end clothing, bags, belts, workout wear, etc. We find and cherish our favorite ones, whether they be Chanel, Louis Vuitton, Prada, or Lululemon. Hell, there is even a black market with knockoffs of the real stuff so that we can chase that label even if it's out of our financial reach. Our love of labels might put a huge dent in our monthly budget, but the pride of walking around with our new Louis bag outweighs the despondency we feel when we see our credit card bill. We love how the labels make us feel special, wealthy, and "high society".

Take Lululemon, for instance. We will spend $125 on a pair of leggings that aren't made with some unique fabric or spandex, but we feel more fit and sexier with a pair of Lulus on than we do running around town with a pair of leggings from Target. Our belief is that the world will perceive us in a certain way based on our designer clothing, and we just may think about ourselves in an elated way when we wear it. I succumbed to this, but remember, my underlying, insidious preoccupation was my bigness. I could afford lovely Lulu, and the spandex kept my tummy sucked in, so it was worth it to buy.

Labels don't only come via clothing. Labels can also be internal ones that we can't wear but still want to make sure the world notices, creating an illusion for others to see. For example, the cost of car you drive, your hair, makeup, house size, neighborhood, family, private school, country club, job title, and education—these are all labels we hold dear. Internal labels give us confidence and pride and attitude, helping us carve out a place where we fit in in the world. Labels constitute our status in the world and help others categorize who we are. Except, this is all false—you aren't who you are because of the college you went to, or the type of car you drive, or who you married, or even how big your house is.

Labels are given to us early on by our family, and sometimes, we never fully shake them off, even if they aren't necessarily right for us. Take my friend, Cori, for instance. Cori was put into the "nurturer" category by her father at an early age. Her dad needed her to take on the role of "parent" since he couldn't handle the role himself. In essence, Cori grew up labeled as the "nurturer" and has never thought to question its validity. Is she a nurturer by nature? Or was this label given to her, and she has carried it with her throughout the years, melding it with her identity?

These scenarios happen very frequently, and I, for one, had a huge identity crisis regarding my family. We created a certain dynamic to survive the chaotic environment of six kids, three dogs, countless cats, and a bird. I was the second oldest but took on the "oldest sister" label, as Tara and I were always grouped together. "Amy and Tara" was my identity, who I was supposed to be. As "Amy and Tara" grew up, we had to be the responsible ones, the ones who had the most chores, the ones who couldn't get into trouble, the ones that had to have straight *A*s, excel at sports, and be level-headed and easy to parent.

Labels are full of lies, fantasies and outdated stereotypes. I
was the opposite of the typical "oldest child" label. I was wild,
creative, bold, dreamy, and certainly not a pleaser by nature. I
would hide bad grades at school and wouldn't try hard in practice.
Tara and I shared a room, and my half looked like a bulldozer
plowed through, scattering and piling clothes all over the floor
with an unmade bed to accent the look, while Tara's side would be
pristine. She was an early riser while I slept late. She liked taking
on tasks; I disliked being told what to do. I even hated having to
walk our dog, Sandy, so I would walk down the street and then
just sit for a couple minutes rather than walk him to where I was
told to. I basically gave my parents the middle finger behind their
backs.

Tara was studious, a pleaser, mathematically gifted, quiet,
clean, and neurotically into keeping order in her room and life.
It all seemed to come naturally to her, but it didn't to me. Oldest
Child was a label I despised but could not shake. I knew it was
inauthentic and didn't fit me, but children don't know how to
break out of the molds forced upon them.

If I could go back, I would tell that little girl to be who God
wanted her to be, to embrace the messiness, the creativity, the
daydreaming, and live life based on her truth.

I remember looking at a yearbook of a public high school
around the corner from us. The yearbook was in the Great
Clips, which was a bit creepy, interspersed with magazines and
periodicals. I saw this picture of a kid named Billy Drip, which
stuck with me for all these years. Billy Drip was a senior, and he
wasn't involved with any activity at school—nothing was listed
by his name. The sheer fact that his surname was Drip seemed
to confirm his lack of interests. It's sad to think about him now,
through adult eyes—maybe he was into animals or volunteered at
church. In my mind then, though, if he wasn't talking up his list of
activities, immense teenage doing, he was a loser.

Kids and teenagers aren't the only ones who define themselves by what they "do" rather than who they are. We, adults, tend to justify our existence with the label we feel gives us the most prestige. I am a stay-at-home mom, a working mom, a vice president, the head of the PTA, a gym rat, an empty nester, a baseball Mom, and a fur mom. All of these things are aspects of my life that require me to "do" something. None of it revolves around me simply existing in the world. No one is going to meet a group of people at a party and announce, "Hi, I'm Sarah, and I am a dog lover—that's all." Nor will you tell someone something like, "Hi, I'm Laura, and I struggle to get out of bed in the morning because I hate my life, but I am a work-in-progress."

You mustn't forget that we are human *beings,* not human do-ers. With that, I did an experiment recently at a party I was attending. I started to introduce myself in a whole new way, and boy, did it rattle some fellow partygoers! It became a conversation fire starter because most of us expect to hear the mundane titles of the people we meet. Instead, I said, "Hi, I'm Amy, and I am a lover of movement and a gratitude seeker!" I amassed lots of smiles and comments, and it opened the door to a more animated conversation. It was a little unnerving at first, though, because we have ingrained habits of making sure people know our job title, our college, and/or how we spend our time.

We want the world to marvel at the most positive label we can present, even if we feel like a fraud or didn't earn the label. It's harder to let the world see our personal truths, vulnerability, our flaws, our passions, our desires, or our dreams. So, we leave the weird, ugly parts of us hidden, along with our innermost dreams, because we fear that if the world sees all of us, they will laugh, turn away, and judge us.

While external and internal labels matter to us, none are as consequential than labels slapped on us as adults by others, such as friends, colleagues, and partners.

How sexy does "Blubber Queen" sound to you? Doesn't exactly go with Agent Provocateur, huh? That label was given to me by the very person I was closest to. When I met my future husband (now ex-husband) as a rising junior in college, I was probably wearing a size 12-14 at that time. He said, on our first date, that I was a "big girl". Ugh, that fucking word again.

My face flushed, and as the same old stories about myself and my size started swirling in my head, I spoke up loudly and told him I hated that word. So, he looked me in the eye with defiance and stated, "I will call you 'large' instead."

I'll admit it. I guess I projected that version of me into the world and it came right back to me. Or he was merely an asshole who had just broken up with a girl that was 5'4" and wasn't used to being around someone of my height. Probably a little of both.

We started dating, and after several months, he took to calling me "Blubber Queen", which made my skin crawl and embarrassed the shit out of me. This nickname, which he thought was funny and endearing, lasted for a couple years. I would ask him to stop, but the only reason he finally did was because he said it in front of his brother, and as my face turned the shade of a beet and mortification coursed through my veins, his brother uttered something like, "Dude, that's kinda rude."

Let's just say he suffered from, to paraphrase Jennifer Aniston speaking about Brad Pitt after he did the photo shoot with Angelina Jolie, "a sensitivity chip" issue. I ended up marrying him anyway.

We all have words that were used to describe us that came from other people but stuck to us and within us. I even started describing myself as a "big chick" when people would comment on how fit I am. It was a blatant insult and assault, but because of how I defined most of my life, I embraced that label and reminded everyone who complimented me that I was actually "a big chick" and would have made a great football player with my broad shoulders.

In eighth grade, I remember being at a pool party when the cutest boy in the class, David D., picked some of the girls up and tossed them into the deep end like a cannonball. David wasn't a massive guy, but he was a huge flirt. He approached me, picked me up, then abruptly put me down and said, "You're too big."

Imagine my horror that he just didn't have it in him to throw me in. He could have—he had picked me up easily—but he was being a prick. You know what? His words stung...and stuck that I was big, large, different than the other girls. At that moment, I felt the spotlight on me, envisioning everyone at the party turning their heads and the crowd silences, as his words remained in the space over us for maximum effectiveness. *Yes, Amy, you are too big, not worthy of flirting with.* The desire to be small was so visceral at this moment in my life I can still feel the concrete under my feet suddenly as he dropped me down. His opinion further created the illusion that I was too big. Some fucking little shit eighth grader held an immense amount of power over how I felt about myself. So troubling and sad, isn't it?

We all fall into the trap of labeling ourselves based on other people's opinions, even if they really don't ring true. But why? To protect ourselves? To put ourselves down before someone else can do it for us? What is so sad is that we rarely feel worthy to receive a compliment. We are so quick to downplay our virtues if someone says something nice to us.

Once you realize this habit, you begin to have awareness. Once you start to change how you think about yourself, you stop being so quick to tear yourself down. Easier said than done, right? Nah. That's simply how we tell ourselves we cannot change, that we cannot achieve what we want, that we have too many roadblocks in the way.

We go through life labeling ourselves and those around us to quickly categorize the world we interact with. Yet, they aren't necessarily based on any truth. Our beliefs and thoughts about who we are and what we like and the expectations we place on ourselves were planted long ago by external opinions. The labels which control our lives directly impact what we do, what choices we make, how we have relationships, and most importantly, how we see ourselves. Most of the time, we weren't the ones who created them.

Were any of you reading this told that you were a "daydreamer", to "look pretty and be quiet", or that you were "too much" as a child? I believe that sometimes, in our society, women are taught at an early age how they should act—that our role is to think small and be small. We are told that it's better to be tiny than big-boned, better to be an "acceptable" height of 5'4" than a towering giant over 6 feet. (How's the weather up there, big girl?) It's more acceptable to project a softer voice, be less opinionated, and stand behind your man—to give up any big dreams in order to raise a family and nurture those around you, to stay at home with the kids and embrace the laundry, dishes, diapers, and play groups.

*Act small, look small, and smile!* Sound familiar? Women, by nature, are softer and more pleasing to look at, wouldn't you agree? When you think about the feminine mystique, you picture curves and softness and roundness. Long, flowy hair, hourglass figure, perky tush. Men have hard lines—squared off jaw, broad shoulders, big hands. As a result, little girls come to believe that daintiness equates to femininity, muscles are for body builders, and being cute and bubbly is the way to make friends. In adulthood, we grow up to be paid less for the same job. We are taught that it is classless to raise our voice, to be bold and speak our opinion. Cussing is "unbecoming" on a woman, but acceptable for the male half of our species. I confess, I've overtly dropped a few choice phrases in here as a fuck-you to that tired notion!

Don't get the wrong impression—my story is not about men being the enemy, or men at all. Far from it. I freakin' love men and who they are and what they mean to us and our world. We, as women, tend to be our own enemies. We have been holding onto ideals passed from our mothers and grandmothers and society that not only keep us from achieving our purpose and finding inner peace but also, perpetuates the cycle, as it is the only way we know to raise our girls.

We spend our lives seeking our next "crack hit" when we feel unfulfilled in ourselves, spending thousands each year on plastic surgery, hair, makeup, clothes, and shoes to feel more "womanly" because we are bombarded by the illusion of perfection every time we watch Netflix, go to the movies, or scroll on social media. One way we "seek" happiness is to chase the perfect body, fixing all the parts we don't like and playing up the parts we do. I am totally as guilty of this as the next girl, so there is no judgment here. I have splurged on my fair share of plastic surgery, Botox, and fillers. I never could develop a designer shoe habit, though, as they tend not to make size 11 shoes.

We all had dreams as a child of who we were going to be before the world got ahold of us and told us to go back into the corner, be quiet, look pretty, and sit/stand up straight. Thus, our little-girl dreams and aspirations were extinguished. We were told to throw water on the fire within us to conform to society. We were told to embrace, internalize, and believe what the world thinks about us and then act accordingly. However, not all labels are negative. To be honest, you may have received labels you didn't think you deserved, but you overcame your initial hesitation and mustered the confidence to accept them.

There are several effects that have been noted in the realm of labeling individuals. The Pygmalion effect is a psychological phenomenon that describes how high expectations can lead to improved performance, while low expectations can lead to worse performance. The effect suggests that people tend to do better when they are treated as if they are capable of success and that their labels and expectations can become self-fulfilling prophecies. This phenomenon has been observed in classrooms, where kids exceeded expectations when they received positive reinforcement and affirmations from teachers, which shows the sheer power that words and labels can have on an individual.

Then there is the Golem Effect, a psychological phenomenon in which lower expectations placed upon individuals either by supervisors or the individual themselves lead to poorer performance by the individual. So, an individual might be told they are stupid and or untalented, thus they will no longer believe in themselves.

Both the Golem and Pygmalion effects are based on external forces, but there is one I think trumps them both: the Galatea effect, which you might know as the "self-fulfilling prophecy". The Galatea effect underscores the idea that those with an unshakeable belief in their capabilities can achieve greatness. Belief in what you want in life, what you can accomplish and knowing you have the talent and abilities to achieve it, is what we all should be striving for in this life.

In the world of parenting, how many of us have labeled our kids as "a great artist" or "a great athlete" or "a great student" so as to push the Galatea effect on them? As we observe their talents and interests, we try and drive home some level of self-awareness of their unique gifts and guide them to focus on what we think they would be good at so they can feel a sense of accomplishment. I tell my kids that if they truly want something in life, they must believe they can achieve said goal and be willing to make the effort to see that goal into reality.

Sometimes, we catch ourselves nudging our children back to the middle, to the safe zone, as we were encouraged to do by our elders. Basically, we tell them what we were told—keep it in the *fairway*. Ever heard that term? It means that you had better play life the way people play golf: just keep the ball on the fairway. Don't go rogue. Don't stand out too much. Don't try a different swing. Just play it safe, and life will be fine. Average. How many of us, as kids, dreamed of an average life? But due to the way the world views us, we begin to believe that we cannot achieve what we truly want, and then we give our kids the very "gift" we were given—the gift of staying in the box.

I am totally guilty of trying to help my children "fit in" to make life easier on them. Sophia came into the world just as I hoped, with creativity and style. This girl was born a STAR! Literally, every day of her life from eighteen months until she was five, she wore a different princess dress, tutu, or glittery outfit. Sophia emitted flair from head to toe. The girl knew who she was and what she wanted to wear and how she wanted to project herself into the world.

Now, mind you, I am also a glitter girl, so I loved that I had a daughter who was obsessed with flair. I gave her, without compromise, the opportunity to explore her sense of unique style, whenever and wherever. But that didn't last. You know why? Because social pressure on her, and me seeing that she was a little too glittery, created a sense of fear *in me* that she wouldn't be accepted. So, as she grew into elementary school, I started telling her to tone down her flair, suggesting she not wear the glitter and sparkles when there was an out-of-uniform day at her private school.

When Sophia was in fifth grade, it all came to a head, as she triumphantly got ready to go to an after-school carnival wearing a unique, flamboyant creation she was so proud of putting together. We walked over to the school, and her "friends" were standing with a group of boys (uh-oh). Those kids laughed at her. I witnessed it, and my heart somersaulted into my stomach. Sophia

went home crying, and you know what I told her? Did I use my
experience to explain it didn't matter what they thought because
she could dress any way she wanted to? *No.* Did I tell her not to let
the world take away her creativity or blow out her candle as Dr. X
snuffed out mine? *No.*

What I said to her was driven by my internal fear that she
would not "belong" and, therefore, would be ostracized and
lead a lonely life. I said, "You need to keep it in the fairway and
stop dressing so outlandish." Again, as Super Flair Mom, I had
celebrated her flair and even encouraged it, so when I told her to
tone it down, can you imagine how confused her ten-year-old self
felt when her mom did an about-face? It scared her. She never
forgot that and still mentions it on occasion. I allowed the world
to dictate how I parented my child and took her panache away.
Shame on me.

We must play a role in this world that is similar to walking
on a tightrope. One slip-up and the world judges you as you fall.
That judgment becomes your truth. And honestly, in my humble
opinion, women are way worse than men. We have this sense of
competition within ourselves that gets projected into the world
because ultimately, we don't want anyone to be as pretty, as thin,
or as perfect as we are, as we pretend to be. Now that is a complex
dynamic, isn't it? We won't embrace and accept our imperfections
because, damn it, that woman in front of me isn't embracing hers
either! Why should I?

Let's talk fair vs. flair in relation to my nine-year-old,
Brooklyn, who I've used the phrase "life isn't fair" with more
than once. If life were fair and we all looked the same, acted the
same, had the same desires, can you imagine how absolutely
bored we would be? So, embrace "life isn't fair" for what it is—it
doesn't matter what is fair or not because no one promised your
life would be exactly like anyone else's. You can't live life feeling
like a victim of your circumstances because you will waste your

life never striving for what you want. What matters to you is that you must embrace the truth that you are solely responsible for creating your life, regardless of the external world. This should give you hope because it means you can change anything about your life that you don't like. That is your power!

How can you change at this very moment? I asked myself this at many moments and visualized my life as a mountain. I am born at the base of the mountain and cared for in basic ways until I can start climbing. As soon as I can walk, I am given an empty backpack and told to start collecting rocks (labels) during the climb. Here's the caveat—I am not alone in my journey. Others surround me—some that love me unconditionally, some that don't like me, some that are threatened by me, and some that are just in a foul mood.

Early on, that backpack will start getting agonizingly heavy as I climb because I am filling it with rocks given to me by others—and there are so many others. Even though I might not agree at the time, I take the rock they give me because they are older than me, maybe wiser, maybe a peer who is more popular than me. So, rather than filling my backpack with flowers and beautiful things (like how I see myself and how God sees me, until the world gets ahold of me) that would be crushed by the rocks, I stop trying to add the flowers and just continue taking the rocks.

Women, especially, are notorious for graciously accepting rocks from others because we are taught that we must be servants to others. We must be nurturers and put everyone else's needs before our own. We are told men cannot multitask, so it's better if we just take on more than ask them for help. We don't want the world to know we are not Superwoman, so we accept the fact that the load we are carrying is our cross to bear.

Those rocks signify expectations, opinions, judgments, stories, and experiences that create our ego. You are well-aware of these expectations written on a chalkboard that only you can smudge up or entirely erase from your existence, wiping the slate clean:

- Get married out of college.
- Have kids.
- Wait to have kids.
- Work before kids.
- Work even if you have kids.
- Volunteer.
- Be head of the PTA.
- Drive carpool.
- Get the kids into the best schools.
- Over-schedule your family in order to keep up with everyone else.
- Accomplish all this while being thin but not too thin because then everyone will think you have an eating disorder.
- Be fit but not too fit because that means you are selfish for spending over an hour at the gym while your poor child has to play with others in the kids' club.
- Dress well, have a full face on, and enjoy spending hours at the park watching your child play in the sandbox.

P.S. If you fail at any of these tasks, you are a bad mom (#*nice label*)!

Many women earn the label of "mom" in their twenties and thirties. Raising children is a frighteningly beautiful experience, as you go from being self-focused to loving another human being so much you would die for them. However, women tend to lose themselves when they are caregivers. Because we are told we are nurturers by nature, we take the label and run with it. We believe we must put ourselves behind all others, even family pets. You often lose who you were before you became a mom or a fur mom or a partner. You forget you are an actual individual that possesses multiple layers and is completely unique. You replace the label of this or that you were carrying and proudly wear the name tag that says "mom".

As a mom, our burning desire is for people to believe we have all the answers, can button up our shirt over those milk-producing boobs (and not show leakage), and that our life is perfect. You take on the new label with no experience, feeling like a fraud because, deep down, you are terrified that God trusted you to keep this baby alive with no manual. You are terrified you will do something wrong. When we allow fear to drive us, we no longer trust our internal voices. Hell, we even start judging other moms and how they are choosing to raise their kids.

Ever feel guilty for wanting to go for a run, leave the baby with a sitter so you can go to lunch with a bestie, or check out a new exercise class at a gym? You think you must put yourself last because that's the broad instruction of how to be a good mom. So, you don't go for the run, you don't meet your bestie for lunch, and you can't bring yourself to put the child in the kids' club for an hour because you think it appears selfish. This "story" you carry, chapter to chapter, written by others, will make you slowly lose yourself.

From my experience, it seems each group must be armed with a defensive shield against the other groups of women— moms vs. childless women, working women vs. stay-at-home women, married vs. single, family-focused vs. me-focused, fur moms vs. non-fur moms, dog lovers vs. cat lovers, workout women vs. tennis ladies, blue-collar women vs. white collar women, black vs. white, young vs. old. We expect to be judged and attacked for the way we choose to live our desired lives. As you now realize the power of labels/words, my ask is that you make a conscious effort to stop labeling other women. It hurts all of us and helps none of us. We can truly do enough damage to ourselves to the point of demolishment or until our flesh and

bones feel like plastic because we're only mimicking a life—a
menagerie of others' imprints.

# Chapter 7

# I. ROBOT



Most of us, through family and society's imprints that were sealed and handed to us in a black envelope, basically didn't have the opportunity nor the courage to be set free in the wild to figure life out. I am not saying that is a bad thing though, because there are some that were guided yet given more room to screw up and try different things, and some would have liked having a little direction.

With the tornado of change and chaos that I stirred up by leaving my marriage, my VP at the time and mentor, Chelsea Tucker, recommended I enroll in a personal growth intensive. While I was clear that I needed to exit this long-term relationship, I didn't know of the tsunami of loss and confusion divorce would dump on my doorstep. To say this intensive transformed me is an understatement because it was what pushed me to find my path and gave me the courage to begin the journey to find my purpose and vision of my future. Holding on to childhood traumas and stories were keeping me from living a life I wanted. I never thought I had the power or ability to buck the system or go against society. The feeling of being stuck, through my fears and traumas, became my catalyst, forcing me to become extremely uncomfortable, but it worked.

During the intensive, the instructor, Cathy, did this
entertaining skit that I will never forget because she was acting out
my life and how I went about making decisions. I was chasing the
idea of finding joy through external things, so the skit really hit
home for me. As a testimony to the need for this intensive, there
were 150 of us sitting in the auditorium as Cathy began describing
what a typical life may have played out for most of the people in
that shared space.

The skit went something like this as I recall: "For most of
your young life, you are completely unaware of your body and
yourself. You love exploring the world, playing imaginary games,
running around the jungle gym, picking your nose, laughing, and
not having a care in the world because life is great! Your world
looks vibrant and fascinating, and you lose yourself in finding
dandelions to which to blow their seeds into the wind, rocks to
throw into streams, sand to build castles with, and so many other
examples. Life before about age 10, to a typical American kid back
then, was filled with wonder at the external world and the things
in it.

"Then at about middle school it hits you: you notice your
body, you notice your smell, you start to want to blend more in
the crowd, start dressing like your friends; no longer picking your
nose in public. Soon, you are quite stressed because it's damn
hard to fit in as the middle school social game becomes more
complex. Your parents went from the kings of your castle, to being
idiots overnight and not worth listening to, as your friends take
the throne. You start to think negative thoughts about yourself as
you compare yourself to how you measure up to others. You tell
yourself, if I can finally go to high school, then I will be happy/fit
in, and life will be great!

"You get to high school, and you continue in the peer rat
race, jockeying to become popular, cool, Homecoming Queen,
Class President, and other special labels. But the social pressure is

so hard in high school, and emotions run high, and you have to do homework and study so you start to fantasize about going to college so you can finally fit in/be happy and life will be great!

"You finally make it to college and living in a 10 x 10 dorm room that smells, studying nonstop, and running yourself into the ground. You decide to join a sorority to find your tribe. But you still feel unsettled and think, *I know what is missing! I just need a boyfriend to make me happy*! You snatch a boyfriend so you can finally fit in/be happy and life will be great! But then feel lost because you are not a kid anymore but not yet an adult, so you start to fantasize about graduating and getting a job in corporate America making a ton of money so you will finally be happy, and life will be great!"

At this point, Cathy started to walk faster around the room and her speech picked up speed. She continued, "So you graduate college with a good degree and a boyfriend and tons of debt perhaps realizing you now have to be somewhere for forty hours a week and take whatever job pays you the most to own your time. You are still not happy or feel like you fit in because now you are completely on your own and can't use college as an excuse for bad behavior. Shit. I am now an adult? You go to work, doing that 9:00-to-5:00 job that Dolly Parton sings about all peppy in her high heels and tight blouse, leading with those triple D boobs of hers. Then you realize life sucks. Your job sucks. You are owned by your boss and who the hell told you this was the best path for you?

Cathy keeps up the skit, saying, "Well, all you need to do is get married so you can finally find happiness! You've been dating your college sweetheart a while so naturally, this is the path you should take. Determined to muster (or damn sure manufacture) contentment, you start planning your wedding so you will finally be happy, and life will be great! Wedding planning and working turns out to be a grind but the day finally comes, and all that time and effort and energy all seems so worth it because you are finally happy! For the moment....

"After the wedding and honeymoon is over and life goes back on autopilot, you start to get unsettled again. You realize marriage is hard, compromising is hard, work is hard, and you start to wonder if this is all there is. Then it hits you. The obvious answer. 'Let's have kids!' Kids will give us purpose and fulfillment and happiness and life will be great! You get pregnant, have your baby and go through life surviving those first few years until it hits you that you still are not fulfilled. You finally say to yourself after swearing you would never go through delivery again, I know, I need to pop out another kid, then our family and life will be great!

"Repetition comes easy. You do it all over again. And another. Then you think, *I will be happy if I lose the baby weight and get down to my high school weight.* So, you jump on the latest diet and exercise program, and it lasts about four weeks because it's too hard to deal with, with the kids' schedules and life being too hectic. Then you begin to think and feel that you would find happiness if only you looked younger, thinner, had a hipper car, more designer bags, a better job, a bigger house, more vacations, more sex, more connection with your partner, more friends, *more, more, more.* Like the Grinch, you seek everything outside of you to fill the void inside you.

"Something in the back of your subconscious keeps nagging at you throughout your phases of life, whispering, 'Is this it? Is this all that life affords? Why am I always feeling like something is missing or lacking? Why am I not pretty enough, thin enough, smart enough, rich enough, cool enough, lucky enough, young enough?' Your subconscious keeps this dialog going because you created that dialog. Yes, I am pointing at you. You created this talk track so guess what? You have the power to discard the whole broken record because it no longer serves any purpose for you in your new life."

Bravo, Cathy! I followed most of the script almost to the point where I became a robot. With no feeling and no joy other than my kids and working out, I was going through life following rules on a path for which I didn't connect with, or feel was mine at all. I did everything I was supposed to do and achieve. Fuck, on the outside everything was good! My life looked picture perfect from the outside,

Part of this predictable path also included staying married "until death do us part". I would never get divorced. I was raised to believe divorce was bad, shameful, and out of the question, and that my life should follow the path the majority of people follow—go to a private high school, excel in sports, go to high-ranking university, study hard, get a good degree, meet my future husband there (preferably someone tall, good looking, and whose family lived in Atlanta so I wouldn't get the wanderlust bug), and date for a good while.

After graduating, I was supposed to work in business, work hard to rise in the ranks, get married, and wait a couple years before having kids. Then, I was supposed to have kids but stay at home with them, get into a play group, talk about my kids non-stop, and then as soon as they could walk, start throwing the ball to them to figure out what sport they would be good at. Then, approximately fifteen months after the first child was born, I was supposed to get pregnant again so the kids would be two years apart.

Coming from a family of six, I never considered solely having two kids—that was too dull of an idea. I needed to have at least three, preferably four, so that there would be no possibility of middle child syndrome. Then, when they were school aged, I was supposed to jump back into the workforce to help pay private school tuition while managing the house and driving carpool. I was supposed to keep date nights going while having kids in club sports on the weekends, going to Church on Sunday, seeing my family, seeing my husband's family, seeing friends, working, working out, and carving out enough time to breathe.

Believe it or not, I did all of *that*. Still, never once was "divorce" mentioned in the perfect life plan for which I crafted the perfect identity to display to the world. That was not a word we uttered. It would tarnish the family name and shout out to the world that I was somehow broken, imperfect, and damaged. I believed it would screw up my kids, create chaos in my life—generally, it would ruin *everything*. So, even as frustration piled up like laundry, knowing I wasn't leading the life I should be leading, I refused to acknowledge that I was unhappy in my marriage.

Fortunately, I picked a man who was a good provider and a very involved dad. But our connection was lost along the way, and the more I pretended in my life, the more I stopped feeling anything. I became robotic—working my ass off, teaching a bunch of fitness classes in my "spare" time, carpooling kids, watching their sporting events, and basically "getting through" my life. When people would ask me what I did for fun, I stared at them like the robot I became. Expressionless. Wow, I knew there was such a thing, but couldn't process what it actually signified for me. Deadpan, I would say, "I work out." They would laugh and say, "No seriously, what do you do for fun?" This time not pausing, I would reply more sheepishly, "I work out." That is how disconnected I was with who God designed me to be. The star. Stars don't grapple with the concept of fun.

I didn't even know what I liked to do for fun. So, I carried the "perfect marriage" label around for eight years past its prime, knowing I was not living my life the way I desired. Internally, I was broken and devoid of emotion—though, no one knew because I wouldn't reveal to the world that the facade I had created was really smoke and mirrors.

A driver for me was that I wanted my kids to witness affection and kindness between their parents, which I still witness with my parents, married for over fifty years. Society guided my choices, despite an unsettling feeling lingering within. I wasn't keen on music class or eager to be the PTA president or library volunteer, yet I pushed to conform. Even when volunteering felt like a chore, I wondered why I couldn't be like the moms who effortlessly juggled tasks. Why couldn't I feign joy while cutting fruit for Girl Scout meetings or find fulfillment planning art projects on rainy Saturdays? It wasn't my source of happiness; it felt like living up to external expectations. I questioned if that was all life had to offer, realizing I might not derive joy because I wasn't meant to fit in that mold. So, I broke my routine, my family, and my life, disrupting my world. I like to say I threw a grenade on my perfect life, in order to create another based on who I am, not what society deems acceptable.

Leaving a marriage carries stigma and none of us go into marriage seeing an ending. Still, there are 86 divorces every hour, compared to 230 marriages an hour in the U.S. alone. Why is there still a stigma when marriages end? I knew that society would have opinions and judgments about myself and the perceived failure of my marriage but even though I heard and felt them, sifted through, I chose to discard them. I did not see my marriage as a failure because I received four incredible human beings for which to raise and nurture, so to me, it was supposed to happen. Now, was I supposed to stay married forever? Was that the path I was supposed to endure? No. I now know that was part of my life that was amazing and wonderful yet, I was supposed to hop, even dance, onto another path that was more of an unknown, one that had not been prescribed for me.

Mind you, I had so many thoughts swirling in my head before I uttered the words, "I want a divorce." Will my kids resent me forever? See me as a failure? My only concern was my children and making sure they felt loved and cherished during the change.

I did have thoughts about how others will judge me and perhaps think I was selfish or crazy. I feared society's thoughts, their whispers, the social media chatter for only a hot minute because in the end, this is *my life*, and I am the one living it every second of the day. I refused to allow fear to keep me stuck in a familiar yet unfulfilling relationship.

After I uttered the word, *divorce*, out into the universe, I experienced an awakening of the Soul and started to gather friends I had collected along the path of life, who loved me unconditionally, to create a circle of support. I knew I needed them during the dark journey forward, as the unknown will always seem dark until you remove the fear. I knew the path would be dark for a time because divorce, even amicable ones, mean change is coming to those you love, and loss always impacts your mind, body and Soul, which causes internal and external chaos for a bit.

I also stopped overanalyzing others' opinions and focused on reclaiming my true self and finding my purpose, alongside prioritizing my fierce love for my children's well-being. Remaining in a robotic, stagnant marriage wasn't the example I wanted to set. I craved to show my kids the tenderness and love I experience daily with my own parents. I refused to let my marriage's construct become their standard. I wanted my kids to see me joyful and content, something I hadn't displayed in years. I wanted them to see me happy and fulfilled rather than robotic.

You know how a caterpillar lives and hits a point where she can no longer be a caterpillar? She painstakingly moves into the unknown, dark chrysalis based on instinct alone. There, she begins to eat herself as she radically metamorphoses into a beautiful, free, flying butterfly. I went through a similar journey, minus eating myself, of course, but the analogy is poignant because you must go through destruction of the old for you to transform into the new.

Change is hard. Going against family and your belief system is hard. Putting down those rocks is hard. It takes a clear intention and mindset to pivot because adversity is hard. That is what forces you to look your life squarely in the eye and begin to question your past and what future you desire. And when you have clear intentions on how you want to live life going forward, it becomes easier to make tough decisions. I knew my focus during the divorce must be on making sure my kids were okay. No one can protect their children from heartbreak, disappointment, or failure, but you can help them work through these things and come out having learned valuable lessons.

I made sure our children still felt loved and cared for, and because of that, my ex-husband and I didn't fight. We don't hate each other. We are great co-parents, and for that, I am truly grateful. Our children are content and settled and thriving, and that was all I wanted. It was a very hard road, though, and there were bumps and cracks during the process, but we didn't lose sight of what was best for our children, both remaining fiercely protective of the kids.

After the dust settled, though, I was faced with a new problem. What is my new identity? I had to become uncomfortably comfortable with my new label—divorcee— and really did not want that label to get put at the top of my identity ladder. *Divorcee* doesn't roll of the tongue well. It's clunky, matronly, limiting. Not that I led with that label while introducing myself. At that point, I was still figuring life out, figuring out my purpose, so I wasn't keen on posting a declaration on Instagram that I was now newly single after being with Steven for close to twenty-eight years. Again, I was cautiously courageous rather than boldly courageous. Baby steps.

Why was I hesitant to shout out to the world that I had pivoted my life? Because I still felt like I had failed a bit and the *failure* label was still one that made me queasy, like something was wrong with me. Never mind that I had successfully created a family life, birthed and raised four kids, with my two oldest getting Division 1 Athletic scholarships and my youngest two following close behind in that achievement category. My kids get good grades, have good friends, and use their athletic ability and personal grit to achieve greatness on the field and the court. All four of them, Cason, Sophia, Colt and Brookie Cookie, are close with each other, conscientious and kind, and are all-around good humans for which I am grateful for every day.

Me—I loved health and wellness, built a nutrition company that was still running on the side, had incredible friends and a nice corporate sales career. The label, *divorcee*, would supersede all my accomplishments, or so I thought. I was still listening to the outside world, looking to it to tell me how to think and feel about myself. Internally, I knew I had made the right decision, but at the time, I wasn't strong enough to block out the opinions and judgments of others.

I am strong enough now, though. And it is the most incredible feeling to hold up your middle finger to the world and say, "I don't give a fuck what you think about my decision. I needed to find myself again and if you don't like it, it does not matter."

I felt like the world fought against me during the process. Get this—I was told by a close friend that I needed to be content with my life, that I should just appreciate what I have and maybe try Prozac to make me happy. She went on to say that I dream too big, and that *normal* life is about being content with routine and to-do lists. She urged me to shift my focus away from me and just do for others, and that should be enough to make me happy. Not have any desire, let alone a desired life to light my fire? Talk about an opinion from someone who has given up or is content living the stock life blueprint many are using.

My dreams were too big and unrealistic? I needed to be satisfied with the mundanity of life? Ever had cold water thrown in your face? It jolts you like a bolt of electricity and wakes you up. What my friend was saying to me, or how I perceived what she was saying, was that I needed to make myself small and "stay inside my lane". Thank goodness I didn't internalize her opinion, but most are not aware that they have power—yet.

I finally found the courage and strength to take "married woman" out of my backpack and place it down, gently. I say I placed it down *gently* because of what it signified. I love the life my ex and I created because it gave me four of the most incredible Souls to raise. Never will I regret one moment of that time. That label meant so many things, and so to toss it out flippantly would not give it the respect and appreciation it deserved. As I placed the "married" rock down, rather than pick up an unfamiliar "divorcee" rock, I envisioned picking gorgeous flowers instead—splendid red, purple, pink, and royal blue petunias to add to my backpack, signifying my beautiful children. The lessened weight on my shoulders signified that, even though it was the hardest change to make, I was lighter and freer than before.

# Chapter 8

# QUESTIONING EVERYTHING BUT DESIRE

> "The desire for gold is not for gold.
> It is for the means of freedom and benefit."
>
> —*Ralph Waldo Emerson*

We collect beliefs like we collect Christmas ornaments—from our families, friends, churches or just from life experience and culture itself. Our young minds absorb everything, forming the foundation of how we understand life. Our beliefs become the filter through which we view the world. Think about the things your family valued—from education, to activities, to moral behavior—they guided how you felt about your reality and what your future was going to look like, and how you act in society.

Ever notice how different people feel about the same thing? I mean, all you must do is examine the political landscape and see how intense belief systems are within individuals. Two years ago, after being so consumed with politics, I decided I needed to step away. I realized it was impacting relationships and taking too much of my mental energy. I began to see that my belief in politics shifted as I scrutinized that industry and how it continues to fire people up. It's a game. One designed to create deep, polarizing beliefs. Yet, when you start to realize that like most big industries, you see it is all about money and power, not well-being or becoming the best version of yourself.

Once I eliminated that focus, my energy shifted drastically. It took some time to pivot, but I do have to say, my anxiety and stress level dropped way down when I stopped following politics because I understood that beliefs aren't necessarily hard truths.

Challenging our long-held beliefs feels like trying to reroute a river. It's hard because our beliefs are so tied up with who we are that it's like questioning a part of ourselves and figuring out what's true. When we question our beliefs, it can feel like we're questioning ourselves as people. It's like untangling yourself from something that's deeply woven into who you are.

I believed that to finally love my physical body, I had to be a certain dress size or scale number. For me to arrive at that number, I needed to follow diets as calories in/calories out, then cardio would sculpt and frame the number perfectly. These beliefs did not serve me one bit! Yet, I clung onto those beliefs like a kid clinging on to her pillowcase full of Halloween candy.

For another example, take my friend, Cori's belief about teeth. She felt self-conscious about her "big teeth" yet when she mentioned it, I hadn't noticed until then! Sure, her teeth were big, just like mine. The crazy thing? She saw this feature as a negative, probably because someone made fun of her teeth when she was younger, and she has held on to that belief since. That one comment altered how she felt about herself and she has spent her life shying away from smiling because she carried the belief that since she saw her teeth as big (a negative), then society would judge her accordingly. Me? I love my big teeth! My parents spent thousands fixing my mouth with braces, so I'm proud of my smile and am often given compliments on my big smile. See how a single opinion can totally change how we see ourselves? See how a "belief" is simply an opinion you have internalized and created a narrative that it is the truth?

The theme of this book is *big desire*, so I wouldn't be authentic if I didn't talk about how religious institutions played into my life just as big business like the diet and fitness industries stepped on my desires. Any industry that holds salvation over your head, making sure you conform to their rules and tithe, accordingly, must be at least mentioned. I, for one, am deeply spiritual and do believe in religion as a way of giving people community and sense of purpose. However, now, I do not blindly believe everything the Church tells me. I became open-minded and understand others who abhor religious institutions and feel they actually stand in the way of a person's relationship with God. I do not judge or have opinions about how someone relates to or against religion because just like all areas in life, what is desired for some, is harmful to others, so keep that in mind.

Many grow up and feel guilted into conforming within a religious structure and told to believe everything the institution spoke as truth. Religion is probably one of the earliest beliefs you were given as a child if you grew up in a family that belonged to a religious organization. Then imagine challenging the religious beliefs that were woven into the fabric of your upbringing and basically defined you as a child. It's not merely a rejection of theological theory; it's a reevaluation of your place in your family (black sheep?), along with losing part of your identity. It's a pretty big deal to turn away or challenge religious beliefs. Also, going further, because we carry certain labels with us, such as "I am a...Catholic/Christian/Muslim/Jew" if we challenge or reject the religious beliefs we were given, we also are rejecting the community attached to the religion, so in a sense, we lose our place in a tribe.

I drank the Catholic Kool-Aid, having been raised in a Catholic family, going to Mass weekly, and going to school from first to twelfth grade in a Catholic school. My identity was a proud Italian Catholic obediently going to church every Sunday and during the week throughout my twelve years of Catholic school. My "belief" was that you had to check the box by going to church, kneeling, standing, praying the "Our Father", and performing all the rituals that go into the Mass. I was taught that God and Jesus were way high up in the sky, separate from me and the priests, saints, pope—and all other religious laypeople were in my way, judging me before reaching God. I never questioned the belief. However, I always had trouble connecting to God. I believed in God and Jesus and the Holy Spirit fully; I just didn't know how to personally pray or speak to them. As soon as I would close my eyes, I would begin the stock prayers I memorized, which left me feeling a bit robotic, followed by a pleading prayer, "Please protect my kids, my parents, my siblings…"

Catholics are not taught to read the *Bible*, and in the Church, for example, there aren't copies in the pews. This fact dates back long ago when the Church wanted to control the message. I would hear snippets of the *Bible* from the two readings and the gospel but did not know how to ingest and believe in the powerful *book*. But I sure believed in the Church, the teachings, the rituals and the guilt as a whole ensemble. That guilt is a real powerful deterrent. And being so firm in my faith of the Catholic Church, I knew when I started having kids, they would be baptized Catholic and raised Catholic. After all, that was what I was and how I planned their future religious growth.

My "belief" was that Catholicism was the best religion out there because it was the only one I was exposed to, and it was the first created. Naturally, as I had children, I wanted to raise them to be good, little Catholics also, which included always going to church on Sundays. Except, I didn't take into consideration that my kids were their own people, with their own thoughts, perceptions and stories of the world around them. I thought that if I taught them to believe the Catholic Church was their only option for their spiritual development, that they would use that as a foundation for the way they build their lives.

As my two older kids made their way through Catholic school, they each approached the Catholic religion quite differently. Sophia was and is incredibly spiritual and independent of me or her dad, always trying to evolve and deepen her relationship with God. And I say this is "in spite of the Catholic Church" by the way. Having to go to Mass twice per week and sit through religion class did not influence her personal spiritual journey in a negative way. The way she has created and maintains to this day, an intimate relationship with God, is purely her choosing. One day when she was thirteen, Sophia explained that she believes Satan can never be on the same level as God because he is not God. He is and always will be beneath God because he chose to separate himself from God. Therefore, the struggle between good and evil isn't God vs. Satan. The struggle between good and evil is between God trying to protect his children and Satan trying to take the Souls of God's children. That hit me so hard because all my life, my belief was that God and Satan were equal. Sophia helped me begin to form a deeper faith and connection with God and for that, I cannot thank her enough.

Cason, my oldest, tells a different story, however, with regards to being raised Catholic. He questions *everything, not just religion.* To this point, we thought he had a syndrome called ODD or "oppositional defiance disorder". It's legitimate—ODD is a term used to describe kids acting in a very stubborn and challenging way. They tend to disagree with rules and authority figures like parents, teachers, or other grown-ups (but in his case, not his football coaches funny enough). Kids with this type of reaction are always saying "no" or "I won't do it" to almost any instruction or request, regardless of the situation. Like when I told him I was going to plan a family ski trip. He replied, "Why?" The typical reaction would have been, "O-M-G, yes, Mom!" That isn't how Cason thinks, because his mind immediately flew to the cost of the trip, the logistics of getting across the country, etc. He was always saying "why" to things he was told in order to literally understand the "why" and once it was explained, he would choose to believe/agree or not, if it made sense to him. I wish that like Cason, I had questioned everything...or at least some things, like Dr. X's tainted prognosis.

Imagine our surprise that one night, when Cason was in tenth grade, we discovered he was questioning his faith. We were sitting at the dock of my in-laws' lake house, chilling on the boat, gazing up at the stars, and enjoying the peaceful feeling the night brought us. It was around 10:00 p.m. at night and you could hear the crickets and water moving under the boat and dock. I can't recall how we landed on the subject, but somehow, it came up that Cason was questioning religion. He said that being forced to go to Mass twice a week "created a feeling of monotonous pomp and circumstance". He started to think that being forced to listen to Mass to "talk to God" at a specific time and specific place each week, was creating separation between him and God. At the time, I literally started to panic, thinking that if he doesn't believe in what the church told him to believe and what I told him to believe, it would be detrimental to his Spirit. That is how my belief and story about which religion must be practiced, was able to control my thoughts and feelings.

Organized religion is outstanding for the community, and if it helps you become closer to God, yet, it can also drive away people so it should be based on your own self and what brings you to a higher spiritual level. Through understanding and being open minded, I have come to grasp what Cason confided in me four years ago on the dock. It wasn't that he didn't believe in God—he perceived that organized religion deadbolted too many constraints on him and his relationship with God. I am proud of my son. Knowing now that all I must do is close my eyes, quiet my mind and begin to speak to God, He hears me and answers me, as I am open to listen.

Your strong spirituality does not mean that your faith won't ever be questioned. Having faith throughout life when darkness hits is easier said than done, especially when you're living it. Take pregnancy, for instance. I know many women plagued with infertility, even with the advances science makes. I experienced a mixture of both, so I can speak on all levels. My first two kids came easily. It didn't take anything but going off the pill to get pregnant with Cason and Sophia. I thought, *if I want four kids, I get four kids*. God was probably laughing at my audacity because Colt and Brooklyn became a game of wills.

With Colt, I had some trouble. I was lean at the time, having gotten into the groove of life without dieting. I was in top shape, but my body fat dropped to about 14%, which is a tad low for a child-bearing female. I developed *amenorrhea*, or loss of your period. It's common in women athletes training at high intensity. It's not dangerous, but if you want to get pregnant, you need everything working properly.

For a year, we tried after I stopped breastfeeding Sophia. When nothing happened, I went to see an infertility specialist. I saw two because I didn't like what the first one told me. Dr. Gloom said the only way I could get pregnant was to stop exercising for four months. That wasn't an option! Exercise is part of me, I love movement. I needed to find another way.

I found another doctor, well-known in Atlanta in the fertility world and an ultra-marathon runner. He said I could keep exercising and tried something unconventional to raise my progesterone levels. He inserted the progesterone pill inside me instead of having me ingest it orally. After one month, my period returned, and a couple months later, I got pregnant with Colt.

Brooklyn, on the other hand, was my "miracle baby". After Colt, I knew I wanted a fourth, especially a girl so Sophia would have a sister. Once again, my period didn't return after nursing. Time to see Dr. Calhoun, a legend in the Mannino household, having delivered my four younger siblings, and all the females in the family went to him. He knew my mom was Fertile Myrtle so just to get a better understanding of me, he suggested a new fertility test. It came back at 0.03 out of 10. At thirty-six, I was told I was infertile.

Two and a half years later, at my annual check-up, I asked about receiving an IUD, just in case. Dr. C told me to come back next month for it. That month, Brooklyn was conceived. Seeing that blue line on the pregnancy test brought me to my knees, as I was about to put in the IUD to prevent pregnancy. It was as if God were saying, "Well, Brookie Cookie, we best get you in there before the opportunity shuts down." That was the moment I realized the power of God and prayer and having faith. Science had no explanation, but I do. God is in control, and we are along for the wild ride.

It can be so scary and wild. I've treaded a winding road full of potholes threatening to take me out in the quest to reshape my belief system. I began to understand how "cognitive inertia", which is the resistance to change entrenched in our thought processes, plays a pivotal role. On a biological level, our brains are wired to seek familiarity and coherence, and altering deeply ingrained beliefs disrupts this equilibrium and causes internal physical chaos.

For example, attempting to modify the belief that success is exclusively tied to professional accomplishments might trigger cognitive dissonance, which happens when the mind resists this internal conflict, preferring the comfort of the familiar belief system.

I was elated to comprehend that our beliefs are not fixed; they are malleable, and understanding this can help you redefine who you are and who you want to be. It requires courage to question the beliefs handed down to us, to scrutinize them in the light of our own experiences. It's a process of self-discovery, where we discern which beliefs serve us well and which hinder our progress. Sometimes, if it goes against your family's beliefs, challenging the belief might also impact your relationship within the family unit and your role within your family. Therefore, it is not an easy task, but honestly, will set you free.

How do we begin to challenge our old beliefs or beliefs that hold us back? Cultivating open-mindedness becomes crucial on this journey. It involves recognizing that beliefs, while influential, are not absolute truths. The ability to embrace new perspectives, question old paradigms, and adapt our belief systems allows for intellectual and emotional growth. My philosophy is ABG—always be growing. Being open-minded to the possibility that what you used to "believe" doesn't have to be set in stone allows you to shift your belief system once you recognize it no longer serves you.

Let me refer to my tried-and-true example for changing fucked up components in life that do not serve us. Dieting, for instance. You were told to believe the only way to lose weight is calories in/calories out. Or you were told the way to lose weight was to get in 1 hour of cardio per day. You believed that, and thus, your thoughts and behavior mirrored that belief. Did the concept of "calories in/calories out" lead to permanent weight loss? Probably not because that is a very outdated belief.

The next frontier I had to explore is what I would call my "stories", or memories that play over and over and over in your mind and guide your perspective of reality. Stories act as threads connecting our past, present, and future. These narratives aren't just memories; they are tales shaped by our surroundings, age, relationships, and the emotions we feel. Stories are personal views, subjective lenses through which we view our self-created reality. Whether positive, negative, or ordinary, these tales etch themselves into our minds, becoming guiding forces that influence our lives.

Our life journey has many twists and turns. The only constant in your life from the time you come into this world to the time you leave is that you are, at your very essence, your Soul. Our bodies change all the time. You are not the same body as you were yesterday, or even an hour ago. Your cells are dying, and your body is creating new cells, new skin, new pathways in the brain. To limit yourself due to past stories makes no sense anymore. If you still use your past to define who you are now, even though you are not the same as you were yesterday, how are you evolving into who you are supposed to be? The allure of living presently, through the past, confines us to an ideal that no longer exists, which weighs us down and prevents us from recognizing we have the power to change. Honestly, who can compete with the past, as it is just perception? Like those guys who can't seem to move past the glory days of high school football, as their present lives never live up to the myth. They are stuck in nostalgia, which deters them from living in the now.

Also recognize that there are three sides to every story: yours, the other person's perspective, and the truth. See if you can explore that as a means to challenge those stories. It's crucial to recognize that the stories we internalize form the foundation of our decision-making but are not 100% true, which is why eyewitnesses to accidents "remember" different scenarios. We often move through life unaware of the subtle narratives we run in the background of our mind, shaping our choices. We unknowingly accept our views as facts. I recall a marketing guru once said, "People seldom believe what you tell them. They rarely believe what you show them. They sometimes believe what their friends tell them, yet they always believe what they tell themselves." Makes you pause, doesn't it? Because if what we tell ourselves is what we consider "truth", yet my truth can be wildly different than your truth, then who is right?

Stories are like records playing in the background of our mind, driving our behavior and our beliefs in ourselves and the world around us. Typically, people can remember some of the "stories" from age five and above that shape the direction of our lives, like Dr. X shaped mine. If only I had been four!

One of my friends, Brandon, was seven when his parents got divorced. It was a terrible situation, where his father walked out one day, leaving Brandon and his three siblings behind. At that time, he decided in his mind that he wasn't "enough", and therefore, his dad left him with feelings of abandonment and insecurity, of which became a huge story in his life from that point on. His Mom struggled to make ends meet after the divorce, so he decided he would never be in a situation of "lack" with regards to money. The story he created in his mind was based on a child's view of his reality at the time. Did his father abandon the family because he was not worthy and therefore, had to prove his self-worth? *No.* That was his perception. The reality of the situation was that his parents did not get along and perhaps neither was happy or content in the marriage.

Brandon went on to be a driven, successful business owner but acknowledges that he still feels the sting of abandonment and struggles to find inner peace. The story he created in his mind played over and over to make him prosperous, but it never removed the feeling of not being enough, which is how powerful stories can be to drive our adult lives.

Going further, as we reach our teenage years, we tend to have the epiphany that we are "different" than other people, and we think individuality is a bad thing; parents stop being our focal point, and peer acceptance rules our lives. We do not want to be different—we want to fit in, to blend, to be part of the herd. We try hard to be just like other people, mimicking their clothes, hair, and attitude as we begin to shed the childhood innocence of unawareness. Or some of us realized early on that we didn't fit the "normal" mold, no matter how hard we would try. So, we embraced the opposite path, diving into being strange. Still, that was a way of fitting in—fitting and blending where we could.

During the adolescent stage, you begin to internalize other people's opinion of you, and these opinions can drive our thoughts. If you don't really know who you are (and honestly, what 12-year-old kid does?), you start to take on personas assigned to you—oldest child, middle child, baby of the family, smart student, great athlete, very outgoing, extremely shy, reserved and quiet, bookworm, hyperactive, obnoxious, etc. We hold onto the stories and internalize the labels, which then prevents us from living our authentic lives. We stunt ourselves.

Emotions come in waves and can appear out of nowhere or triggered by your thoughts. When emotions are strong, they can rapidly play general and overwhelm our thoughts and cloud everything. Think about Romeo and Juliet. Their love was like a whirlwind, influencing everything they did and consumed them completely. Sometimes they matter more than logic or what we deeply believe so you could potentially say emotions trump beliefs and thoughts? Either way, emotions are part of being human—sometimes big, sometimes small, but always there running in the background!

My ask is that you become a "dreamer" again complete with the emotions attached and old stories removed from your subconscious mind. At what age were you told to no longer dream, to get your head out of the clouds, to focus on school? It's a different age for everyone but use my story as a kick in the ass to go back to your inner child's mind and let your imagination run wild.

It's a beautiful thing to watch my nine-year-old, Brooklyn, do this with horse figurines. Brooklyn and her besties, can play for hours as they take on the characteristics of the horses, using books to create stables and Barbies to play the roles of riders.

My oldest daughter, Sophia, was the queen of imagination play. Along with her best friend, Lola, they would dress up as village girls, go outside, and spend eight hours climbing trees, drinking tea, and making up a world they wanted to be a part of. Their level of visualization and focus in creating a world they controlled and believed in, always amazed me.

See, I believe it is through imagination that God places ideas and visions into our minds and through our individual talents, we take the vision and create something physical in which to impact the world. This concept of imagination is relevant if you have ever been to a gallery opening or festival where artists are showcasing their creations. One summer, I was at a festival with my friend, Jason. We were walking around, looking at all the booths set up by vendors, and I suddenly became overcome with emotion as I felt I was looking at God's gifts. If you start to open your eyes to what is around you (not constantly distracting yourself with your phone), you begin to be in awe of what surrounds you, noticing the beauty that others are showing the world.

What made it so impactful to me was that every single booth had different paintings, different art in unique styles. And if you begin to realize that your creativity comes from a higher source (in my case, I believe God gives us creativity), then you start to realize that we all are given gifts. Those gifts manifest in different ways based on our experiences, exposures, and desires, but each of these artists possessed a vision of what they wanted to create, and that vision began in their mind with a thought.

Each one of the artists started with a blank canvas. Each one picked up a paint brush. Each one picked the first color they would start with. And each one created a one-of-a-kind masterpiece to exhibit. Do you think, if they had sat down at the blank canvas and said, "I suck at painting/I'm not good enough/ People will judge me/I don't have time to do this silly painting" that the world would have ever seen their beautiful painting? No way.

So, even though they all started with a blank canvas, these people intentionally created art from a vision they had within, which formed a thought, which became an action, which then became a piece of art they chose to show us. Each booth was so different from the last, which makes it even more incredible because these artists felt compelled to create and then were vulnerable enough to share their work with the universe. *Wow!* Talk about having the balls to put yourself out there. To be judged. To have the world's opinion as the gavel. Yet, they believed in themselves and had the courage to share. We need to live our lives like artists, showing our gifts and our vulnerabilities and being authentic in our lives every single day.

Being vulnerable and authentic is quite difficult when you are busy trying to live life based on society's view of how you should live your life. Most people fear being vulnerable, exposed, judged. I was like that for most of my life, allowing fear of failure, fear of being different cloud my journey. However, I learned that bravery could walk hand in hand with fear. It simply had to, or I would fade away in the darkness. Like other thoughts, fear is habitual, keeping you up at night or from your desired life. How long do you succumb to a belief or projection rather than act, take a step? The very nature of life is vibrancy, not dimness.

# Chapter 9

# FEARING MY FIRE



It's no longer a secret that most of my decisions in life were based on what society and my family thought I should do, and on overdrive from the belief system I was given, with a huge helping of the powerful emotion of fear of failure sprinkled on top. I put myself in a self-created *box*. This box, which most freely stay in because it's a known and familiar, is what prevents us from awakening to what our true purpose is in this life. We are told to fear other countries, fear war, fear recessions, fear car accidents, fear disease, fear head injuries from riding a bike. Fear keeps us in our box for sure which is by design, by the way. I would love to know some statistics from the 70s and 80s about head injuries from kids riding their bikes. Somehow fear was pushed on us and now if you see a kid riding a bike without a helmet, you are going to severely judge that mom for allowing such a flippant act to occur! What about plastic bags? You wonder how many kids suffocated by putting a bag over their head? It might have been one or two, but by goodness, that narrative was shoved down our throats and printed on every plastic bag in America.

As you experience life, you collect fears along the way and store them nicely in the self-imposed box you have created for yourself like a keepsake box. This box holds our beliefs, our stories, our thoughts and our emotions, and then dictates our actions through movement and words. Within the box, everything is basically entwined together making everything so much more complex. Because emotions are so powerful and have a vibrational frequency, the powerful emotions usually take center stage.

The concept of vibrational frequency of emotional states is real and documented and isn't some New Age woo-woo idea designed to create hippie communes. To start, did you know that we are *energy*? Before last year, I did not pay attention to this field of science, having had my fill from my time at Georgia Tech, but suddenly I became fascinated by it. Quantum physics tells us that the human body is made up of both matter and energy. The energy is chemical (reactions within the body) and electrical (signals and impulses). Science has proven that our physical body, our thoughts, our emotions and our spirit all emit emotional frequencies outside of us. You know when you are standing there and just have a sense someone has walked up behind you? You can't see them, don't hear them, but you sense their presence.  It's their energy field you sense. So damn cool to think about! Those mood ring makers were onto something, weren't they?

The concept that our emotions and thoughts are energy was mind blowing to me. The saying, "feel the energy of the crowd", takes on a whole new meaning and actually gives you a sense of power because you chose to emit a low emotional vibrational frequency (anger, hate, rage) or a higher frequency (joy, happiness, love) every day without realizing you are the driver of the energy force. Think of an ice cream cone (because I love ice cream!) as a visual for emotional energy. If you start at the top of the cone, where the opening is the most expansive, you will find that enlightenment, peace, joy and love emit the greatest energy frequency into the world. Move down the scale, lower frequency emotions like anger, fear, grief, apathy, guilt, and shame manifest within, keeping us feeling stuck, hopeless, and miserable. Understanding the vibrational frequencies of emotions is empowering because emotions don't just impact our mind, body and Soul; they influence and impact those around us. Ever hear the saying, "You can smell their fear?" In essence, we can sense the presence of someone's emotion. We cannot see it, we cannot hear it, we cannot touch it, nor can we smell it (unless it hits you as stress-induced BO). What we can do is *sense* the emotion. And when we sense a positive or negative emotion, we tend to internalize it ourselves, judging if, based on our stories and beliefs, we should take on the same emotion from that individual.

Fear is palatable and thick and can drive an individual to stay in their self-imposed box of a familiar hell. In my case, fear of heights lived within me and prevented me from climbing up rocks and looking over cliffs. Don't judge, but even walking up floating stairs in houses sent my central nervous system into panic! One of my earliest memories of fear of heights was when I was about six years old and went to my cousin, Katy's house, for Christmas. My aunt and uncle were renovating their house and adding on a second floor. Katy's room was on the second floor, however, and the stairs were still under construction so there was no railing on either side between stairs.

A normal person would walk up the stairs, maybe towards the middle, but would feel confident stepping *up, up, up* to the top. Me? Gripped with fear, I remember seeing the open sides and the space in between and not being able to pick my foot up on the first step. Even after watching Katy going up and down the stairs gleefully, I could not move. In a moment of brilliance, Katy told me to crawl up the stairs so that my body never left a step. I crawled slowly up and quickly got away from the drop-off with a sigh of relief before the fear of not being able to get down hit me suddenly. My dad had to come and carry me down as I gripped tightly to him with my eyes closed. That story, buried deep in my subconscious mind when I was six years old, stayed with me into adulthood where I automatically responded with "I have a fear of heights" to any situation that might involve climbing. I was allowing a program, built into me as a child, to limit my experiences I could have as an adult. Makes you wonder how many other self-limiting beliefs are preventing you from living?

In my journey, I've come to understand that fear isn't a tangible enemy, but a story we tell ourselves—a narrative spun from threads of "what if" and "I can't". It's the voice that whispers we're not good enough, not ready, or not worthy. This self-created emotion, devoid of factual foundation, can clip our wings before we even attempt to fly. How many sunsets have gone unseen because we feared the height of the mountain? How many friendships never blossomed because we dreaded rejection? How many dreams have withered on the vine because we couldn't bear the thought of failure? Fear doesn't protect us; it imprisons us and can rob us of joy, growth, and experiences that make life more colorful. Yet, the good news is that if we can create fear, we also hold the power to tear it down. Our subconscious mind can be reprogrammed. This explains why we all pick different fears up along the path of life. I have a fear of heights but for others, they thrive on adrenaline-filled activities like jumping out of an airplane! Would I ever want to jump out of an airplane? Nope, not on my bucket list—more like my "Fuck No List". I did lessen my fear of heights by going to the Grand Canyon and hiking down and back on the narrow strip of path, with nothing between me and a 500-foot drop. If you could see me now, I am patting myself on the back.

Fear is not all bad though and is a normal part of life, when it is kept in check.  Did you know that babies are born with only two fears: fear of falling and fear of loud noises? All other fears we pick up along the way and for some, we can use fear as a roadblock for pursuing directions and stepping outside our comfort zones.

Some fears are tangible and based on past experiences. For instance, if you have a fear of dogs because as a child you were bitten by one, well, that is a tangible fear. Or, if you almost drowned in a pool when you were young, you might have a fear of water. One of my besties, Jersey Jen, has a well-known fear of flying. She can't recall when the fear took root, but her whole adult life she has had to deal with this inconvenient fear for which she has no idea how to get over. She has flown twice in her life, and I was…lucky (maybe not the right word!), to be there for her when she took her second plane ride. I did not judge her, nor did I try to talk her off the ledge. I was simply there providing support, telling others to give her some space as she took some Benadryl to calm her nerves (and knock her out). I can't say my hand was ever the same, the way she was gripping it during takeoff, but the level of anxiety and stress this emotion caused her was quite remarkable and eye opening to me, and I could feel it.

Can you imagine what emotions she was dealing with, what her thoughts were, and what kind of chemicals were being pumped throughout her bloodstream? The fact that she was able to put one foot in front of the other was a feat that is nothing less than incredible. See, what got her on that plane was a bigger driver than the fear of flying. In Jersey's case, she loves her job, and we were flying across the country (no way she could drive) for a yearly company meeting and she needed to be there in person to accept her award for her exceptional sales numbers. The drive for achievement was greater than her fear of flying. Notice our fears do have a hierarchy. If you ask Jersey to fly for personal reasons, she will say, "That's a hard no for me." But if it has to do with her career, which she has built from the ground up, she will somehow make it onto the plane.

Think about it like this: Fear does not exist outside of ourselves, it is the meaning we choose to assign to a thing or situation and that meaning is stored within our subconscious driving decisions and experiences throughout our lives, if we allow it to. I like calling it "worst-case scenario thinking", which Steven was prone to do. And when you are around someone who has a specific fear, you tend to start to internalize that fear also, so it's an unwanted gift that keeps on giving.

I was raised in a household that didn't lock doors. I mean, based on my mom's opinion, we had dogs which were the No. 1 deterrent to crime. When I met Steven, he was raised completely different. From a military family, he was raised in a more intense environment, keeping a knife in between the mattresses just in case, never sitting with his back to the door, and other nuances. For me, this was foreign, as I was never programmed with the belief that there are so many threats out there.

Imagine how hard it was to change my belief system to reflect a fear that wasn't ingrained in me. You might say, why would I internalize the fear he created in his head? Well, hear me out. Can you imagine if I chose to reject one of his fearful beliefs and something happened? I didn't take on the worst-case scenario fear; I created the "what if" fear within myself and it was magnified when I started having kids. *I mean, what if the pacifier dropped on the floor and there wasn't a way of washing it off?!* What if someone didn't wash their hands before holding my precious newborn? What if the car seats weren't installed correctly?

Fear of the unknown is so powerful that it drives you to think, feel and act a certain way because it will never go away. You will never be able to conquer fear of the unknown until you pinpoint the fear and then try it if it is tangible or flush it, as it is holding you back.

Now, don't get me wrong, I had *plenty* of fears I created on my own. For instance, I believed that I had to graduate from Georgia Tech no matter what (there was never an option to change schools) and the fear of flunking out drove me to studying harder and longer than if I had gone to a "party school". On a foundational level, the fear of my parents' approval, or lack thereof, was a huge driver for me. In essence, it wasn't necessarily the fear of failing classes at Tech; it was the fear of what my parents would think if I were a fuck-up. Huge motivation for me to get my ass to class and participate in study groups.

I never questioned if that was the right school for me, and I never questioned the direction I would go after. I assumed I would get a job in corporate America and work for a salary with weekends free. I never thought to question if this life direction would fulfill me or allow me to use my talents. The blueprint was already completed for me and was pretty standard. Problem was, I am not the norm; a bit of an outlier, but at that point in my life, I was trying to fit in and be small or basically pretend to be someone else. Once I started working, chasing external fulfillment or ideals, I felt stuck. Ever heard the term, *sunk cost*? This concept basically means that I was already so far down the standard path, my time and energy already spent going in this direction, I felt that I would never recover that time and needed to just keep going.

Why are we so programmed to stay stuck or continue down a path we know isn't right for us because we look at it as a sunk cost? I think I know why: because our central nervous system, the system designed to keep us alive, wants stability and routine and familiarity and is not there to help you grow and expand. Your brain literally would pick a familiar hellish situation, over an unfamiliar future because at least you know what you are dealing with.

"How do you get unstuck and go against that internal driver that is designed to keep you safe?", you ask. Removing fear of the unknown from your thoughts and thinking more like your inner child. You do this by becoming aware of these self-limiting thoughts playing on *repeat repeat*. It takes a shift in perspective of the situation, catching these autopilot thoughts, stopping them, and changing them. By doing this mental exercise, you will begin to rewire your conscious mind with new thoughts.

For months, I have studied the mind and how the body holds onto emotions and the most insightful lesson was seeing how powerful the subconscious mind is. Most of us sometime during school were taught about the difference, but did you ever stop to really understand the power of both? The conscious mind operates in the present, aware of your immediate thoughts, emotions, decisions, and actions. So, when you are deciding which route to take when you are driving, or what to make for dinner, your mind is working on solving those issues.

The subconscious mind is the driver of our lives, however, and is how we can somehow drive to work without remembering anything about the trip (we have done the same thing for so long) or the fact that we breathe, digest food, pump blood throughout our bodies, without having to consciously think about doing so. We run on autopilot most of our day, which should make you pause and think about the movie, "Groundhog Day". Bill Murray must repeat the same day over and over again until he finally receives his manifestation right before leaving the loop. I loved that movie but realized how true to life it really is for a majority of people.

Here's a kicker. By the age of thirty-five, most of us are basically Bill Murray, reliving the same day over and over. Our routines are set, our thoughts on repeat. It's how we get stuck, how we let society control us. We choose predictable over spontaneous, and our personal growth pays the price.

Did you know your subconscious controls 95% of your behavior? Holy shit, right? It's storing all your past traumas, beliefs, and society's expectations. It's shaping your reality from the moment you wake up to when you hit the pillow, based on the past, and we don't even realize it.

The wild thing about the subconscious? It doesn't judge. It's like a computer, storing everything without questioning if it's true. Your thoughts and emotions, whether good or bad, color your perception of your current reality, even though these thoughts and emotions might have been stored there long ago when you were young. Yet, we are still allowing these thoughts and emotions to run our lives as adults. With emotions like fear, our subconscious mind buries these deep inside us, yet they influence our actions without us even realizing. We have become adept at trying to gloss over the nagging feelings that make us uncomfortable, which is why when you are feeling unsettled, scrolling through mindless TikTok or Instagram can help push those feelings down so that you don't address them. Does it distract much?

Fear of the unknown is at the root of all fears, whether tangible or intangible and emotions are the bridge between our conscious and subconscious minds that keep those thoughts around fear alive and well. Fear, especially, shows up in our dreams, letting our subconscious work through our anxieties. I had to learn to rewire my subconscious to change my life. Visualization became my go-to tool, creating mental images of what I wanted, paired with positive emotions.

Another trick? Rapid Transformational Therapy. It's basically lying to yourself, but it works. Most fears aren't even based on real experiences anyway. I used this to handle a sticky situation that had to do with rollercoasters and Brookie Cookie, who is an empath and in tune to my emotions. Meaning, if I am happy, she feels it, if I am stressed, she feels it as well. When she was eight, we went to Six Flags, and she wanted to ride on the rollercoaster desperate to experience the thrill. Me—I am not a huge fan but my fear of being a bad mom overtook my fear of heights (remember there is a hierarchy of your fears).

We got strapped in and started up the ramp and at that very moment, Brooklyn regretted her decision and looked at me with tears, screaming, "I want off!"

Knowing there was no way off the ride, that we would be enduring the whole ninety seconds of sheer terror, I made a split-second decision that I had to pretend to *love* the experience because I did not want her to experience pain. I smiled big at her and put my hands over my head and yelled, "Baby, this is sooo fun!" In essence, I was talking to myself, affirming, "This is fun, this is great, this is exciting!" because my body was panicking. I knew if I told myself this lie enough times, my body would take the cue and then Brooklyn would not feel the fear vibration from me; she would get the joy emotion from me. It worked like a charm. Did the roller coaster lift me out of a fear of heights? Not entirely, but success begets success, and we need to celebrate the small victories. Did it cure my fear of heights? Not completely. But it dulled it, reshaped it a bit. I celebrate that small victory. Sometimes, facing your fears head-on is the best way to start dismantling them.

I could talk to my inner child about this fear of heights, but I had more important self-esteem business to tend to.

# Chapter 10

# MEETING WITH INNER CHILD



After my cosmic shift from my comfortable life to the wide-open unknown life, I was basically desperate to stop feeling scared and frozen, looking for external fixes, and I was at the point that I would have tried a lobotomy to stop the thoughts and feelings I was having. I had no regrets leaving my old life, but I was also totally freaked out because nothing in my reality was the same. Pretty much every aspect was dismantled: my house, my job, my schedule, my time with my children, my identity, my comfort. Throughout my life, I tended put a wall up and then run from my feelings because I was never taught anything different. When someone says "lean into" your feelings as a way of healing, I would outright laugh at the concept. I want to *run away* from my feelings, not sit in them and allow them to marinate. Stemming from me pivoting away from my "white picket fence" life, all I knew to do was mask the feelings of fear, disappointment, and lack of clarity in my path. The personal growth intensive and playback of my life, courtesy of Cathy's skit, opened my eyes to vulnerability, authenticity, and healing, not from a weakness perspective, but from a growth perspective. It sparked inside me a glimmer of something profound: hope.

As I became curious about healing the inner child in me, I started to crave knowledge. Knowledge, not from the conventional angle or mainstream angle that is standard when someone has a problem, but knowledge regarding alternative ways of handling anxiety, stress and fear of failure, which stemmed from childhood and beyond. I didn't know it then, but I was having a crisis of identity, and my "identity" that I showed the world for so many years was suddenly no more. Talk about an internal crisis. Suddenly I realized I was carrying many rocks (labels) in my backpack that I had mindlessly picked up and lugged around with me, which had no basis on who I actually was. And I was worn out. I was tired and felt lost because if I wasn't the Amy that I presented to the world, who was I? How do I begin creating my own path without taking into consideration the opinions and judgments and rules I had always lived by? Do I trust myself enough to make decisions based on me and the path I didn't have the courage to take way back when?

I began seeking and searching for ways I could heal my five-year-old self, twelve-year-old self, nineteen-year-old self, and all the other ages that stick out to me as years where I felt lost or afraid to be authentic. I had that sense again that I was uncomfortable in my own skin and wanted to run from myself. However, you cannot escape YOU, so rather than continue to mask, I stopped, stood tall and told my inner self I would make it a priority to spend time learning, growing and healing. I had never stopped before. I was raised to be a "grinder", work my ass off and fall asleep less than five minutes after my head hit the pillow. Rinse and repeat. Rather than take the advice of my friend, who suggested Prozac and lots of wine to self-sooth and fall asleep, I began to think about other ways of handling my raw emotions and thoughts churning in me, which was prolonging the time it took for me to settle down and drift into sleep. Amy sans sleep is not ideal.

So, I did what I do best—took action to find a solution to my stress that was impacting my sleep. I Googled hypnotherapy sessions, scheduled a consult and looked forward to seeing if this approach would find its way into my subconscious programming to begin my healing. The hypnotherapist I first met was well-known in his field. We talked about what was happening in my life and what I wanted to gain from getting hypnotized. I asked if he could just erase all the touchy memories, stories and thoughts that were too painful to marinate in so I could move beyond. He chuckled softly. I said I was kinda joking, but not really. I asked if there was a way like "spot erasing" painful thoughts and feelings while leaving the warm and fluffy ones. At the cost of $8,000 for 8 sessions, this hypnotherapist would help me move past the feelings, help to reprogram my subconscious thoughts and give me a new direction and lease on life! Sticker shock hit me like a brick and the hope I felt with this new concept quickly deflated me.

After picking my jaw up off the floor, while my heart raced and panic started creeping in (this was the magic bullet but holy shit, I couldn't afford that!), the hypnotherapist said he could recommend someone else in his practice that would be a little more wallet friendly, Daniela, aka Dani Kortava, specialist in neuro-hypnotic repatterning.

I clicked immediately with Dani. Not only was her voice soothing, but she also had an inner calmness that radiated outward. My concern was that I did not want my personality changed, all my memories removed, and any hocus pocus you think about when the word "hypnosis" pops up. Dani assured me hypnotherapy wasn't about erasing your past in bulk. It was about reaching a level of calmness in your mind, where your racing subconscious mind can be subdued and the subconscious can be reached so traumas stored deep within, can be uncovered and brought into the light.

Our conscious mind works to solve problems in real time during the day.  Then, when we go to sleep, our subconscious mind takes over to process and store relevant experiences, thoughts and beliefs. The subconscious mind is deeply linked to our emotions. It's the part of our mind where bold feelings, such as fear and desire, are processed and held. That is why I was so drawn to reach this area of my mind because if I were to create a new path for my life, shedding the old beliefs and stories weighing me down was the strategy I needed to follow, and rather than take a drug or go to talk therapy, this way was different and unconventional, kind of like me.

According to Dani, hypnotherapy helps you reach into the subconscious mind, and begin to change habits, behaviors, feelings and thoughts. We started our first session where Dani started asking me questions about why I was here, what I wanted out of the sessions, how I was feeling and why I was feeling that way. Most of the session was what I would consider "therapy", as I described my past and present and Dani absorbing these details to craft the message she was to give to me when I went under. With fifteen minutes left, she told me to close my eyes, lean back in the comfy, plush chair back, put my hands on my stomach, and breathe deeply and slowly.

As she began to help me relax, I started to go into a state where my thoughts grew quieter, and my body began releasing the stress I was holding. I didn't realize how I was holding the stress through my shoulders and other parts of my body. She recorded the hypnotherapy session for me to use at home. I was pleasantly surprised I felt calmer when she brought me out of it. I was the same person, not a walking zombie, yet I felt more peaceful and calm.

I continued my sessions with Dani because each session helped me calm the chaos and worry and fear I had created, with my uncharted path of life I was now walking on. Never in my life

have I ever felt this level of relaxation and calmness. I surrendered
to the process with every part of me—mind, body and Soul.
However, it was still expensive—not $8000 expensive—but with
a sizeable price tag that I knew I couldn't afford to continue once
my six sessions were completed.

The tremendous gift hypnotherapy gave me was that it
opened my eyes to the possibility that I could harness the power
within myself to heal myself without relying on pills, alcohol
or a therapist. Dani, through her insight and guidance, gave me
courage and a sense of control and was one of those people God
put in my path to help me see my world differently. Never had
I been so open-minded. The craving to seek answers, as I began
realizing my own power within, was another experience that
led me further into the new life I was intentionally creating. My
whole life I did what I was told to do or frankly, what I thought
I was supposed to do and finally, during this time, I gave myself
permission to visualize unconventional paths available in this life.

After those sessions, I began being inquisitive about the
subconscious mind but like most things, life is still coming at you
100 mph so even with the sessions, I stopped expanding on the
idea of reaching past my limiting beliefs. I continued to use the
recorded therapy sessions as a way of calming my mind and body
down right before sleep and that was life changing for me. The
sobering realization that the last five to ten minutes before you
drift into sleep are the most critical moments that will impact your
dreams and what your subconscious processes from the day should
wake you up!

Now, I am not telling you to run out to get a hypnotherapist,
unless that is something you want to explore. What anyone can
do though for free is protect the last ten minutes of your day,
before you turn the light off to ensure your thoughts and beliefs
about you and your life, are positive and in tune with the direction
you want to go in. Trust me, your subconscious mind only listens

to your voice; thus, you have complete control in what you are feeding it. Talk about power! With all things though, one and done isn't going to cut it. There must be repetitive exposure to these recordings and messages you tell yourself to truly influence your subconscious. Most experts state that at least thirty days is needed to have an impact on your subconscious mind. The aim is to shape the subconscious mind during the sleep state, harnessing its receptiveness to create lasting changes in thought patterns and behaviors over time. This, in my book, became a concept worth its weight in gold.

# Chapter 11

# BIG TRAUMA



One of my best friends, Megan, had a vastly different upbringing than I did. Her father was raised modestly but driven for more, achieved success in his career and as a child, Megan lived an opulent life with the big houses, horses, and limo rides. However, when her parents split, Megan's world was transformed from excessive wealth into apartment living so the shame of her environment caused extreme trauma to her and started her tumultuous relationship with money, or lack of money.

Throughout her adolescence and teen years, she seesawed back and forth between her mom's apartment in Key West and her dad's estate on the East Coast. Eventually, as her Mom drank more, she was sent permanently to live with her father and his new wife back into the abundant lifestyle. Talk about messing with a child's world. Megan's trauma was not only money related but also, feeling abandoned from her mom who chose alcohol over being a mom.

When I was told of her background, it seemed like it could be a screenplay. Yet, here she stands, with an incredible life she has built for herself and her three boys, escaping more traumas along the way, including her father's death when she was only in her 20s. What most don't know is that she had to do intense internal work to shed the feeling of fear of abandonment and lack of abundance in order to create the life she desired. She is a badass female and was one of the first friends I called when I decided to divorce Steven.

Personal trauma, regardless of its scale or when it happened, holds equal significance to you. It could range from the loneliness felt as an only child to enduring various forms of abuse during childhood that, even as an adult, still makes you feel victimized. The core message is this: Every individual carries their unique trauma, stored in the subconscious, shaping emotions and thoughts unless confronted and addressed.

Before last year, I would have felt silly saying I suffered from childhood trauma because again, in general, I had a normal upbringing. My parents were married, I had siblings, a cozy house, dogs, cats, food, friends and the opportunity to dance and play sports. My opinion was that any emotional issues I suffered should not be compared to those individuals, like Megan, who had drastically different and harsher environments they were exposed to as children.

My fear of being big, fear of not getting good grades like Tara, fear of being left out of my friend group, fear of failing in sports, fear of being rejected for my size at dance and of course, fear of not being seen caused such internal distress and anxiety that I caused trauma to take root. However, if you were to compare my fears to Megan's, you would probably say she wins the award for hardest childhood. In the land of fear and trauma, though, no awards are given. If you experienced fear and trauma as a child, you are in the club, regardless of the degree, and not one of us escaped childhood unscaled.

I remember being in the labor and delivery room, facing my fear of having a large needle jabbed into the back of my spine to numb me so I wouldn't feel the pain of delivering Cason, when the anesthesiologist walked in. I told him I wasn't sure I wanted the shot because of my fear I would be paralyzed. He said, "There is no medal for pain, I do this every day, so you might as well get the injection while I am here now so you can enjoy your baby when he comes out!" That advice stayed with me.

Fear and emotional trauma often hold hands. When we face trauma, especially in childhood or from experiences that shake us, fear can become a part of our everyday reality keeping us stuck and frozen. Trauma is like a ghost that lingers in our subconscious mind, influencing how we react consciously to situations that remind us of those painful moments. The emotion of fear becomes tangled with those memories, and it can influence our choices, reactions, and even the way we view ourselves in the present.

Experiencing trauma isn't just about physical hurt; it's also about emotional pain that sticks with us in our stories, our buried emotions and our reoccurring thoughts. Not one of us has ever escaped this type of trauma because if you were a child and teenager, you suffered some type of emotional trauma. It can be feeling left out or unseen as a kid. Trauma of not making a sports team, or of having too many expectations piled on you. Feeling like you're not good enough for your job, your life, your spouse. This kind of experience can really change how you think, feel, and act and can rear its ugly head when you are navigating life as an adult if you don't face it head on. When these small or massive events happen, they leave a black mark on us and color how we see our reality. They can make us doubt ourselves or create fear that what happened in the past will repeat in the future. We are all basically carrying invisible rocks in our backpacks and these past traumas hide within our subconscious mind to cause chaos and basically can do a complete "mind fuck" on you if you don't become aware. (That's not a medical term so don't quote me!)

During my awakening, I began to really notice many were using the term, "childhood trauma". Because our parents don't have a manual on how to raise perfect kids, they operate as best as they can. Same with their parents, and the parents before. We cannot protect children from trauma, whether it be from a parent or friend, or a stranger but we can help them navigate their reality so that the trauma doesn't turn into fear and guides their decisions and life from that point forward. We are all on this Earth together alongside good people and bad people. You cannot bubble-wrap yourself or your loved ones. Therefore, every single one of us has trauma we suffered when younger. There are different degrees of childhood trauma, so when we hear horror stories of depravity and dysfunction, we think, *Well, my childhood was a breeze compared to hers...* But your subconscious stores your trauma without comparison or judgment, so your trauma isn't being compared to someone else's trauma.

I talked about a life-changing "story" that became the foundation of how I saw myself. That fucking Dr. X. Now, if I ask my mom, she believes that is exactly what Dr. X boldly stated: "Watch that one, she's going to be chunky." But really, who knows how the conversation went? The perception was that he thought I would be overweight as an adult. Notice I said "perception". He might have started talking about people in general, how the rates of sugar diabetes were rising when discussing sugary foods. I have no idea really—I was only five. Still, I took that story, and the opinion of some random doctor, and began believing his perceived opinion of me, was the truth. I allowed one man's flippant comment to determine the path of my life (for a while). That happens all the time to children because adults are seen as authority figures and thus, tend to know more than a child. As children, we look up to adults. But adults sometimes mumble words in passing, never realizing that a child will internalize the comment and begin shifting their view of reality. Consequently, because we live around and with other human beings, we all get subjected to some form of childhood trauma during our young lives.

Sometimes though, kids can go through dark times and get positively impacted by an adult. Parents lacked a manual on perfect child-rearing, and our lives intersect with countless others, each leaving their mark in either a positive, neutral or negative way so all of us probably have sad stories or stories that were traumatic but that someone swooped in as the hero. It's a good lesson to absorb because you never know the impact, positive or negative, your words and behaviors have on another human being, especially on kids who are forming their identities. There is also lightness that emerges where trauma exists, which can shape the story of someone's life.

Such a story exists surrounding my father, John. My dad was a volunteer coach for my younger nine-year-old brother. My dad is a very charismatic guy, quick with a smile and a calming force that others gravitate towards. That season, there was a player on the team named Christian and unbeknownst to my dad, he was struggling that year. Christian was having a tough time that fall after his dad left his mom. During that football season, with a void and loss in his life, Christian found that my dad filled that fresh gap his own father had created and said he changed the direction of Christian's life. How did I come to know that my father's thoughtfulness and kindness as a football coach would deeply affect Christian? Life's synchronicities unfolded as Christian reappeared in my adult life.

Our boys, both around the age of nine, shared the football field, as Colt, an impressive athlete, played quarterback on the same field my brothers had played on years ago. During these games, my father, resembling his younger self, stood among the spectators as Colt performed incredible feats. Christian recognized the man who had greatly influenced his life—a figure he'd needed during a challenging time. He approached my dad, seeing his former coach, shook his hand, and marveled at this unexpected reunion. Later that day, Christian revisited his childhood memory box, finding a photo of the football team with my dad, a beacon of light during his darkest hours. My dad, unaware of his profound impact, was humbled as texts were exchanged detailing how my dad saved him that fall. This taught me that our influence on others can be profound, even unknowingly. Living authentically and striving to be our best selves can create lasting impacts on people we know and people we meet in passing, especially on children.

These internalized stories silently shape our behavior, defining our understanding of ourselves and our approach to life's challenges. Whether conscious or not, the stories we tell ourselves hold significant power. However, these stories are just narratives based on your perception, opinion, and feelings at that exact time you hear them. Yet, we mix them into the very foundation of our lives; we call them truth. And it's hard to not fall victim because children's minds are like sponges—they soak up experiences and new adventures, other people's opinions of them, how life is, what to expect. We were all children once, thus the emerging term, *childhood trauma*. No one escapes, and everyone gets a medal.

# Chapter 12

# PROCESSING THE SPOTLIGHT



"Desire is the starting point of all achievement, not a hope, not a wish, but a keen pulsating desire which transcends everything."

—*Napoleon Hill*

Before my divorce, I only tried once to see a therapist to help me seek answers regarding why I felt uncomfortable in my own skin and that was before my wedding day. Steven didn't believe in therapy and no one in my family had ever uttered the words, "I need a therapist", because like I mentioned, we all felt we had a normal upbringing and had the roadmap of our lives already charted and "therapy" was like a dirty, secret word. This wasn't uttered out loud, of course, but in my mind, it was taboo to proclaim I needed help in an area of my life that seemed out of balance. Have to be perfect in the light, right? And needing therapy meant I was less than perfect. Growing up with a mom that was Superwoman, she could handle any type of chaos thrown at her all the while nurturing her young humans and dogs, teaching fitness classes, kept us fed, made sure our homework was done, picked us up from carpool line (always the last ones standing there waiting though), and more. She was basically a sheer force able to handle it all; thus, demonstrating weakness was not something I wanted to be seen as having.

In that first encounter, I didn't go for talk therapy but to see if I should go on Prozac, way before my friend told me to try said pill. I felt like I was losing my personality and was so stressed while starving myself for the wedding. I went once to a psychiatrist who asked me a couple questions like "Am I going to harm myself?" (No), "Am I losing interest in food?" (Haha, big no), and other routine questions before writing a script for Prozac. Problem was, I felt such shame to take the medicine that I got it filled but was too afraid to take it. It was like I was considering the bottle as a red pill/blue pill situation the "Matrix" surmised. If I took the pill, I could never go back to pretending to the world and myself that I was struggling. I would have to admit (*gasp*) that I was having a hard time understanding my thoughts and feelings. Well, turns out I didn't have to really make a choice because Steven found the prescription and asked for an explanation, as shame colored my cheeks a bright red color. That was it, because the amount of embarrassment was overwhelming. I told him I hadn't started taking it and that I would throw the pills away. I did not want my future husband to think I was crazy and thus, never tried after that. I felt such shame that someone had seen inside me to know I wasn't perfect, that I struggled, that I was weak and to me, that was unacceptable.

Shame is like that voice in your head that tells you that you're not doing things

right, that you're somehow not measuring up to what you should be. It's feeling embarrassed and small, as if you're not meeting the expectations of the external world—especially the ones you think others have for you. Guilt, on the other hand, is the feeling you get when you believe you've done something wrong. It's like a heavy weight on your shoulders, making you think you're to blame for things not going well, or that you cannot control yourself. And then there's self-loathing—you as your own worst enemy—and hating who you see in the mirror. Such a debilitating act when you look at yourself and feel really negative about who you are, what you look like, and cannot see the bigger picture of who you are. You might focus on your flaws, real or imagined, and end up thinking you're just not good enough, not pretty enough, not thin enough, or don't have enough followers on social media.

In my early twenties and thirties, I was not around people who were open about having to go to therapy because mind you, that would mean you are admitting to be somehow damaged or broken, and my carefully created picture-perfect life had no room for that label. I guess the people I hung around with were either going to therapy and not wearing this on their sleeves, or were like me, unable to believe that their unhappiness or feeling that something was missing was part of the course of life.

I found myself tearing apart my so-called "perfect life". Like ripping off a Band-Aid knowing the pain would be swift yet needed, I bid farewell to a twenty-three-year marriage and the cozy comforts of a palatial house and a dual-income household, along with the constant companionship of husband and kids. No sugar-coating it, my world turned into a whirlwind of chaos. Stepping out of my warm, snug cocoon, I ventured into the unknown. It felt like sinking in an unfamiliar sea, burdened by the weight of it all. I yearned for an expert to rescue me from this abyss. My worst nightmare? Facing epic failure and admitting to the world I was flawed. The fear of regretting my leap from security to unpredictability haunted me relentlessly. When I uttered the words, "I want a divorce", into the universe and Steven, I ended up going to a therapist during the entire divorce in order to talk through my feelings and emotions. I had become more open minded by that point in life, and although I only told my closest friends about Morgan, at least I was making strides recognizing I needed help.

These talk sessions were good, but I never left there with a clear path forward, which I was seeking. I felt a bit talked out, so that's when I decided to shake things up and try something different—somatic therapy. No more chit-chat therapy routine for me. It was time for a radical change. Somatic therapy is based on the idea that the things that happen in a person's life, including negative experiences, are not only stored in the brain but in the body as well, and through techniques, these memories can be brought up the surface from where you feel them in your body, allowing you to acknowledge them and eventually, release them out of the body.

My encounter with a somatic therapist blew my mind. She understood me, she saw me, and all I wanted was that—to be noticed and understood. The irresistible feeling felt familiar, explaining my gravitation towards dance, the spotlight, and my first transcendent experience, which I describe earlier in the book. I was a nine-year-old, dedicating myself to the dance troupe, always hidden in the back row, when suddenly, everything else seemed nonexistent. The stage lights morphed into a single, radiant beam, shining solely on me. Everyone else, the audience, my fellow ballerinas, all seemed to fade away. It was just me, basking in the gentle warmth of the spotlight. I was overtaken by peace, joy, and a sense of delight as I danced with all my being. It felt as if God were there, acknowledging my presence with the perfect words, "Amy, I see you, you are loved immeasurably."

That extraordinary experience is etched in my heart, forever, as you can tell, and I travel back to that moment frequently. On probing into it, my therapist figured out my childhood longing for attention and to be seen for who I was, not seen as who I was supposed to be. Maybe it was because of growing up in a house brimming with siblings and pets, where calm was a rarity and we worked as a unit, less like individual people. It was always "Tara and Amy," not just Tara. Maybe I felt ignored when my brother, John, was born, as he was a terror, crying all the time and destroying Barbies, toy trucks, my Dad's record collection. Nothing was safe with John Boy around!  Maybe as much as I loved my younger siblings, Leslie, Christi and Mikey (and eventually John, of course *lol*), I held resentment towards them on a subconscious level because they took my parents' eyes off me.

Uncovering this narrative and understanding where the trauma sat, in my gut, was revolutionary to me, and that experience made me feel recognized by a greater power. Having this revelation, everything made sense. All my life, I'd been driven by this fear of being invisible, yet the bigger I became, the more I wanted to shrink and vanish. My coping strategy was to blend in and be small, when all along, my Soul wanted to stand out, to shine.

There is a concept called "looking glass self" introduced by a sociologist named Charles Horton Cooley, who believed that our sense of self-worth isn't just about how we see ourselves, but also, how we believe others *perceive us*. It's like building a puzzle of yourself using pieces from how you think others see you. So, when someone says something mean about you (*You have a big nose!*) or treats you in a certain way, that can affect how you feel about yourself and it can devalue how you see yourself. Say you are eleven years old and someone tells you that you are butt-ass ugly. You might internalize this comment and begin to create your life using someone else's opinion, walking around the world thinking you are hideous. Powerful, isn't it? Words matter, of course, but we freely *allow* random people or family or friends to *shape* and define how we see our reflection in the mirror and then due to pressures faced to fit in, we begin projecting that reflection as truth.

This was really evident when I was with a friend, Matt, as he was describing his thoughts about himself and the psychological trauma he endured as a child. This was a man who played baseball from the age of five and beyond, was a phenomenon when it came to pitching hard balls, started as a freshman for his high school, won a scholarship to Florida State and was drafted during college by a minor league team. My opinion of his past was that he was a gifted, driven elite athlete and made it farther than 99% of the population, yet he speaks about feeling like a failure because that is what his father always told him throughout his life. His father was brutally hard on him as he tried to live vicariously through his son. This pressure to be perfect and feeling that no matter what, his father never approved of, stays with him still to this day. Never mind, he has an extremely successful career, loyal friends, and beautiful kids. He saw himself only the way his father saw him way back when as "less than" and unworthy. How many of us do this to ourselves? We internalize the expectations of others and allow our lives to be controlled. Our thoughts then become how we are lacking, rather than how we are successful.

What you are seeking, internal peace and happiness, is never outside of you, and recognize you have the power to minimize the traumas that have kept you stuck or in fear for so long. Your mind only listens to your thoughts, so when you decide to finally filter your thoughts, catch the negative ones that do not reflect who you are, you start to move ahead in your journey of rediscovering you.

Assuming you love your family, your husband/partner, your children, your routine, your friends, your job maybe, you continue to seek something to fill an empty void that lingers because what you are searching for is the true essence of *you*. Material things are something we want, but listen closely—purpose and passion are what we seek to fill us on the inside. Recognize your value and self-worth internally is the first step towards healing and should not be impacted from anything outside of ourselves.

# Chapter 13

# MORE SINFUL
# THAN VANITY



"Knowledge is the eye of desire and can become the pilot of the soul."

—*Will Durant*

As young girls, we are not taught to understand who we are and what should be the driver within us. We are told to be quiet, sit down, get in line, cross our legs, follow the rules, be good little girls. Unfortunately, we take this to mean we need to pretend we are something we are not. Same happens with boys in school. Boys are naturally touchy, physical and need to move around. They learn very differently than girls yet, our school systems are designed around teaching to the female student, the one sitting nicely with her ankles crossed and pencil ready to take notes. I always feel sorry for boys, as biologically they need to wrestle, fight and feel their physical world and the typical school ignores their needs.

Society is constantly telling women how we should act and behave because let's be honest, this gives others more control. With groups of people, there has to be some semblance of calmness so rules are needed. We, though, internalize the *rules* and opinions, and try to mold ourselves into what society thinks is the perfect female. The way we act, look, walk, talk, move, think. We are seeking our whole lives to fit in to the Martha Stewart homemaking ideal, mixed with Margo Robbie's beauty, Jessica Biel's body and lips, and Angelina Jolie's rebellion and charity work, all molded into one. We never question if we would want to fit into a construct that doesn't serve us nor helps our individual talents shine.

Which is why women might begin to develop an identity crisis as they look at themselves in the mirror. Who wouldn't if you were routinely told as a young girl to be a certain way and act a certain way and of course, look a certain way. Some women openly reject society's opinion of what they should look like and chart their own path. Some women try to fit the mold with extensive plastic surgery and fillers and "skinny shots" to lose weight. And some women become very myopically focused on a specific body part in a negative way that will then morph into something far different than reality. Basically, they come to believe that their identity and self-worth is defined by their body or parts of their body that they deem unacceptable and yucky.

This type of thinking becomes like unwelcomed weeds, as thoughts will take root inside your head and begin taking over your daily behavior, creating a complete and utter mess within you. This is called *body dysmorphia*, and it consumed me, swallowed me up, particularly in my twenties.

Body dysmorphia, the opposite of body confidence, is like a plant that feeds on the negative thoughts and opinions of societal beauty standards. The constant glare of social media, comparing yourself with friends and peers, overtakes all rational thought you have during the day. You start obsessing about how to cover up the parts of your body you find unfavorable or ugly based on what society has told you. These negative body thoughts mess with your head and can impact work, school, and relationships, breeding social anxiety, loneliness, an unhealthy obsession with plastic surgery, and worst of all, self-harm.

If you've ever experienced a brush with body dysmorphia, it's like having an annoying scratch on your phone screen that you can't ignore. Only, instead of ruining your viewing pleasure on YouTube, you're stuck with this idea that your belly looks like the Pillsbury Doughboy, and this image plays over and over in your mind, and convinces you that it's all anyone can see when they look at you. Your nose, your thighs, your every perceived flaw. It engulfs you, holding you hostage, dictating which events you grace with your presence, how you pose for pictures, and sadly, even your moods.

You find yourself playing David Copperfield, walking by mirrors, hoping that your stomach would have done a disappearing act like his stage assistants. But guess what? The mirror is a reality check. You are no magician. That damn belly is still there, sticking out like a sore thumb and thus, the endless loop of negative self-talk in your head starts again. There is really no reprieve as you know, mirrors are everywhere, as are images of perfect bodies on screen and on your phone.

I was consumed with body dysmorphia, so I know what it is like. It is all-consuming. I need to name it to tame it. Not only did I despise my stomach pooch; I began wanting to hide my arms, so my closet was designed around my arms and belly. I started covering up my arms in college and became queen of the sweater set. You know the one with the tank underneath and the button-down sweater? I had several sets because I refused to wear sleeveless shirts or capped sleeves, as it would accentuate my big arms. I never really thought to appreciate my shoulders, or my butt or my legs, which were very well-defined. No ma'am. It was my imperfections that defined me and became a compulsion to hide them. Before I go any further, if you've not picked this up in any other part of my story (my REAL story), I want to impress upon the fact that this is extreme behavior and self-destructive.

I look back at photos from my twenties and I still can recall exactly what I was thinking when I see the picture because what I was wearing was quite meticulously thought out. I never would go

out of the house with a baggy sweatshirt (too bulky for my broad
shoulders), or hipster jeans (needed to make sure I wore high
waisted to hold my stomach in) or god forbid, a sleeveless tank that
would accentuate my big arms and expose them for all the world to
judge.

When I was twenty-six, the hubby and I decided to go on a
cruise leaving Miami, to celebrate our anniversary. In August. Yes,
Miami in August is basically like flying into the depths of Hell
since the temperature could be as high as 110. In the shade. Well,
I was about seven years into severe body dysmorphia, having
gained back about 20 pounds from my starving weight before
the wedding, so per my identity, I had to ensure my arms were
covered up because of the dysmorphia.

Even though we would be in a different city where I knew not
a soul, nor the fact that it was an inferno, I only packed sweaters
and shirts with three-quarter sleeves because reason and being
rational wasn't in my wheelhouse regarding my body parts. I recall
walking around downtown Miami, about to have a stroke with my
face flushed and my comfort level at a 2, the heat was so intense,
and I was dressed like it was fall. I did not care that no one knew
me, I did not care that the heat was intense, I thought it was more
important to hide my arms. (You could take that to mean I am
determined or that I don't give up? Kidding!)

Again, even though my arms were not that big, the thoughts
I had swirling in my head created a false reality, which dictated
how I behaved. The typical thought I had the moment I stepped
in front of the mirror was this: my arms are big and thick, cover
them up, do not ever wear sleeveless shirts because people
might only notice those big arms. My breasts are ample so I can't
wear boatneck shirts either, which I didn't even touch upon.
Oh, and don't think about showing your stomach; the bane
of my existence, my pouch belly must be hidden with Spanx

and high-waisted shorts and jeans, even to the point of almost collapsing from heat stroke.

Most women have something physically we don't like on ourselves, that maybe isn't so severe as to be called body dysmorphia, but it is rare to come across a female who loves every part of herself. We are not supposed to think we are perfect as we are made since that is called *being vain* and no woman was raised thinking vanity was acceptable. Yet, why do we teach women that they can't love all of themselves? Again, society wants you to create your identity and self-worth based on their standards of beauty. Follow the money trail and see how much money is spent on makeup, hair, and plastic surgery. It's a whole lotta money and most have jumped at the chance to fix, tweak and cover up our imperfections with the latest products and procedures.

We are told we need to change to be pretty or be seen or to seek complete perfection, which again, is subjective so no one can ever reach that horizon. You could generate a perfect female using technology, in 3D, and tell everyone that you declare her the most beautiful woman in the world. However, there will be many who will disagree because beauty is subjective! We know that on a higher level, but it is so hard to live that concept in our own lives because society's standards surrounding beauty captures the headline.

It's also hard to raise girls in this environment where emphasis is placed on looks (both what you have and what you don't have). My oldest daughter, Sophia, chose to focus on her hair as something she wishes she could change. The Manninos were "blessed" with thick, luscious locks and my boys and sister, Brooklyn, won the lottery in that game. She would say to me, "Why did God give every one of my sibs thick hair and mine is pin straight and fine?" I would say to her, "You always want what you cannot have" and would tell her the story about my sister, Christi, having ringlets and always wanting her hair to be straight.

I would then proceed to point out all the incredible physical attributes she got, like her massive, beautiful eyes and perfect nose. That's what you do for the people you love; you build them up and help point out what characteristics you think are beautiful that they possess and should appreciate more. Honestly, it takes intention to stop the "lacking" thoughts because if you can't change something (the size of your feet, your height or if your hair grows out straight or curly for instance), it's better to embrace and move forward rather than focus on what you cannot impact permanently.

Seeing our lovely parts is hard to do, because the world is out there telling us what needs to be fixed and changed on our bodies. That makes it hard to appreciate what parts are unique and beautiful because, God Forbid, we accept a compliment and believe the person who said it! We are taught that we need to put ourselves down, even when someone sees something beautiful on us or in us, like it would be conceited to accept the compliment! We justify the exchange by thinking they must be trying to be nice, or they probably say that to everyone. I call it "mind-fucking yourself" and my friend, Megan, is the queen of it. I point it out all the time because it pisses me off that she doesn't see her incredible qualities. She doesn't see how beautiful and smart and funny and loyal and strong a woman she is. I see these elegant characteristics she has and feel honored to be in her energy, which is why she is one of my closest confidants. But lordy, she gets the mind-fuck gold medal by constantly deflecting when I compliment her. She refuses to allow herself to think about herself in the way others see her. Now, I point it out all the time because I refuse to let her mindfuck herself and call her out every single time she won't allow the compliment to linger in the air followed by a simple "thank you". That's what friends do—protect you from yourself!

Why are we so quick to downplay strong qualities/features we possess to focus on the ones that we feel are imperfect or we have been told are less than an ideal to have? It is usually based on the stories of our past and our experiences. So, even if you don't have body dysmorphia in the clinical sense, most women have a body part they would trade quicker than it would take to trade in that iPhone for the newest version. *If only we had her legs. If only I had her boobs. If only my skin was smooth like hers....*

Many of us are programmed to disregard and downplay compliments because that is how we are taught. We don't want to be seen as too self-assured. It's a subconscious behavior that is so ingrained in us, that we don't even realize we are doing it until someone points it out.

I started recognizing the need to accept compliments, not only for me, but also, because think about it like this: that person took time out of their day to give me a compliment and I now feel it is kind to just receive the flattery and appreciate their willingness to utter it out to the universe. It does take practice, but when you realize the compliment can positively impact you (if you internalize it rather than discard it), as well as the person delivering the verbal flower, you are more likely to accept the next one that comes your way.

Navigating my twenties amid severe body dysmorphia and the pressure of fitting into societal roles of working, getting married, having kids, and joining clubs, I grappled with imposter syndrome, a common experience. This phenomenon isn't just a whisper; it's an undermining force that makes an individual question their accomplishments and taints self-perception.

I was put in charge of leading a team of sixty sales reps at the tender age of 25 at a startup company. I had worked my way from inside sales rep to project manager and then reached the pinnacle as director of operations reporting directly to the two owners. I was constantly and secretly questioning why they put so much confidence in me when this was my first real job out of college. I felt the imposter syndrome at Georgia Tech since I went there for management, not engineering, so this concept was not foreign to me. I didn't think I belonged at a school like Tech, and I certainly shouldn't be helping run a company! I worried that I couldn't measure up to the ideal they had in their mind of this smart girl who graduated from Georgia Tech. I didn't see what they saw at the time, which was probably that I was a hard worker, competitive, driven to make money and personable. I just didn't believe deep down that I was smart because my brain wasn't wired like my book-smart, engineer-minded, older sister, Tara. But you know what? Fuck the impostor syndrome mentality. Your fight against this mindset starts with acknowledging that there's NO ONE like you. No one else has your experiences, your insights, or your unique voice.

When I started writing this book, my mind was swarming with doubts. "Who am I kidding? I'm not a writer. Who gives a shit about my story?" Then I thought about artists, photographers and songwriters, people gifted at creating something just to make the world smile. In all practicality, does the world need another painting, book or song? Probably not, but that opinion doesn't matter to the person creating.  They want to create something that at the foundation, might have already been produced, but with their own unique spin, feel compelled to share their art with the world.

When you hear a song on Spotify, let's say it's a cover of a song beloved by many, it can excite you because it's a new take on an old song, familiar words but unfamiliar voice. It brings a new presence in the world, gives you a new perspective.  We should give the world our creative products, be it music, art, writing= because that is why God gave us our unique talent in the first place! You realize "sharing is caring" and thus, share your gifts with others rather than hiding them in the dark for fear of judgment.

Not only did I begin writing during my dark time after the divorce. I began learning about things like astrology, meditation, yoga and more outside-the-box ideas about my identity. I came across Human Design, a fascinating holistic self-knowledge system. Simply put, we each possess energy because we *are* energy (remember, I touched on quantum physics earlier). Again, you can feel the presence of someone else behind you before your senses catch on. You felt that person's energy field because we all have energy fields.

Human Design is a system that merges ancient wisdom with modern science, crafted by Ra Uru Hu in 1987. It's not a belief system or a religion but more of a tool for self-discovery or blueprint into how you are. This method breaks individuals into five main categories: Manifestor, Generator, Projector, Reflector, and Manifesting Generator, each defining a unique energetic blueprint by time of birth, birthdate and place of birth. Understanding your energy type can lead to making decisions that are more in tune with your inner self, enabling you to live authentically and efficiently. It also might explain some of the ways you operated as a child and interacted with others. Based on my memories, I always sensed I was different.

From the five energy types, Manifestors, 9% of the population and what I am, are the initiators, those who can spark action without external forces and are considered the creative force in the world, not waiting for approval from society. Generators, 70% of the population, are the workforce, gifted with sustainable energy when they do what they love. Projectors, 20% of the population, are adept at guiding and managing energy without having to do the heavy lifting themselves. Finally, at 1% of the population, Reflectors are sensitive mirrors of their environment, reflecting the energy around them. Manifesting Generators blend traits of Manifestors and Generators, acting quickly but still needing to engage with what truly resonates. They are still considered Generators though, making up a subset category.

There is so much more about Human Design, including profiles, crosses, and defined centers, so I only scratch the surface here, but it can be used as an insightful tool for self-empowerment, helping you make choices based on your true nature rather than societal conditioning or external influences. These categories don't define us entirely, but they provide insight into our tendencies, decision-making processes, and how we exchange energy with others.

Once I found out I was a Manifestor, so many things fell into place about my personality and how I navigate life (even as I did when I was a child). Manifestors inform the world what they are doing, without asking for approval and tend to like having a stage or microphone for which to push their creative endeavors into society. We possess the unique ability to initiate and make things happen. We are leaders who take action and can create powerful changes in the world around us. Kings and generals tend to be Manifestors,

I encourage each of you to figure out your energy because it told me so much about why I crave being able to inspire others through my wellness passion and once you know your energy, it can fill in missing pieces for you, which to me, is incredibly valuable as I carve my path in this world.

# Chapter 14

# CARING FOR THE ONE
# IN 8 BILLION

"A creative man is motivated by the desire to achieve,
not the desire to beat others."

*—Ayn Rand*

Just like astrology or the Myers-Briggs personality assessment, many corporations ask their employees to take, we all are trying to figure out who we are in a world of 8 billion people. So not only do we try and find out who we are and why we act a certain way, as we carry the rocks (labels) in our backpack through life, we now must deal with knowing what the 8 billion people think, feel and act like because we have social media. There is bound to be an explosion of self-doubt, self-worth and self-destruction as people compare their lives to everyone else's. Add the pressure of pushing out perfection through social media. *Damn.* Are we fucked? Not exactly. You are only fucked if you continue to allow the external world to determine your value, who you are and what you desire in life because like, love or hate it, social media is a fundamental part of how society operates.

The explosion of TikTok, Snapchat, Instagram and Facebook altered our world. There are 5 billion worldwide social media users, and the impact of this monster has changed how the world functions. Before social media came on the scene, we had magazines and TV, but their impact on an individual's life was minimal. *Sports Illustrated* "Swimsuit" edition told us which body type was "in", *Glamour* and *Vogue* told us what body type was best for the runway, *People* magazine gave us a glimpse into what celebs were the most coveted, and TV shows/movies gave us a way to escape our lives and be entertained. But again, we could throw the magazine away, walk out of the theater or turn off the TV, so the impact was big but not on the scale of social media with twenty-four-hour access to be voyeurs.

In the era of constant connectivity, where the world is a click away, our perception of reality is shaped by doctored snapshots of others' lives on social media. For young girls and women navigating the digital landscape, the quest for self-acceptance often becomes a perilous journey, as we compare ourselves to others constantly, in what they look like, how they live, what they are doing. It's hard to remember as you scroll if what you see is an illusion, a snapshot or moment posted by another, designed to create a narrative or get you to buy something. Behind the scenes, that influencer still wakes up with bad breath, deals with relationship problems, and has had to stand in the line of the postal store, which is torture. We are human and life is not always rosy or pretty or joyous, and mostly the moments we have are a bit on the mundane side. Driving in traffic, trying to get your kid to school on time, walking your dog, etc. Your friends and the people you choose to follow aren't probably posting these mundane moments, yet our negative chatter comparing our lives to others creates an unrelenting pressure to conform to societal ideals that are not only unrealistic but often unattainable. The impact on a woman's body image and self-worth is profound, as the mirror magnetizes our flaws.

I get exhausted scrolling through Instagram and TikTok because perfection is everywhere, yet, I know that when a woman posts a beautiful picture of her walking on the beach, the "reality" is probably that her husband had to waste thirty minutes of his life using her phone to get the "perfect" shot as she deletes the first fifty he took of her because she looked "too fat," "too old," "bad angled", so she can post her perfect shot, wanting the affirmation, attention of a fleeting heart or like button, from a handful of people who swiftly move on continuing to scroll.

Your picture/video is merely entertainment. It does not inform others about who you really are. The person might make a snap judgment about you or solidify the opinion they have of you, for that brief second, before getting distracted and moving on to the next person's post. You spend minutes/hours of your life to get the perfect shot, and most will see it and keep scrolling and never think about your post again. So why are we wasting precious moments and minutes and hours of our lives trying to show the world the illusion we are perfect?

Don't get me wrong, I am totally guilty of this and will be the first to admit I do like pushing my "good side" to the world. We want the narrative out there that we look beautiful, have glamorous lives and thus, people will be more interested in us, right? Maybe. Aside from that moment in time, captured after fifty bad shots, life moves on for everyone. If we posted pictures of us doing the dishes, walking our dog, picking up clothes off the floor, screaming at our kids to get a move on, it's not very interesting, right? Creating an illusion designed to control other people's judgements and opinions is draining, to be honest, because in the end, the only opinion and judgment you have complete control over, is your own. You can't control how other people judge you or what opinions they have about you or how you live your life or how you look in their eyes or what you do each day to justify your worth to the world. As stated before, everyone judges and everyone has an opinion about you, but it is *not* a reflection on you! Their opinions and judgments are based on their own stories, thoughts, beliefs and perceptions, so if you understand that part, what someone else says about you is a mere projection from them onto you, not concrete truth.

I had quite a teachable moment the other day with my nine-year-old. She had cheerleading pictures and had left her cheer skirt at her friend's house. We didn't have time to go retrieve it. Brooklyn had shorts on, mind you, but was so embarrassed that she did not have the skirt, she wrapped her jacket around her waist. I asked her why she was trying to hide herself since it wasn't like she was walking around in her underwear. She said, "People are going to look at me wearing shorts because I don't have my cheer skirt on." After taking a deep, calming breath, I turned to her and said, "Good lesson, Cookie, because here is a fact: No one cares that you don't have a skirt on because they only care about how they look to the world. They are not thinking or worrying about how you look, so shake it off and own it!"

I taught Sophia, my seventeen-year-old, the same lesson when she was younger. Sophia has always had the cutest bubble butt I have ever seen. My opinion, of course, but ever since she was five, she had a perfectly rounded tush she inherited from the Manninos. However, we all know that if you have some body part that isn't the "norm", you will most likely fall prey to the snarky comments from peers because it's different and sets you apart. In the world of middle school, no one wants to look or be different from the tribe.

Throughout adolescence, we go from being blissfully unaware of our bodies (kids pick their noses, sneeze into food, scream "wipe me" from the bathroom) to being aware of what our bodies look like in contrast to other people's bodies, so when Sophia was eight, she went from being unaware of her bubble butt to being laser focused on said body part thanks to her classmates at the time. During an overnight Girl Scouts trip to the mountains, Sophia and fifteen other girls were going to swim, play games and spend quality time together. That night, while the girls were getting their bunks ready for sleep, a couple of the girls started making fun of the size of Sophia's tush. And then the other girls joined in. Her butt was bigger than the other girls, who were mostly tiny, dainty things. That night, upset and alone on the top bunk, trying to fall asleep, her mind began storing this negativity into her subconscious programming as her self-worth was destroyed a bit by the judgment of a couple of other peers. The next day, she got home and broke down in tears on her bed. As I rubbed her back, she told me what happened and that she wished she wasn't so big. Notice she took the size of her butt to mean all of her was big. *Ugh.* The vision of my childhood came rushing back and I was looking at this beautiful child God had created, and thought, *How do I fix this? How do I help this child understand that her body doesn't define who she is and that those opinions shouldn't matter?*

I wanted to demonstrate compassion and understanding, with an ample serving of insight. In a soft voice, I said, "Sophia, do you realize how lucky you are?" Her eyes bugged out like she had seen an alien.

I pressed, "Do you realize that you were born in the perfect time to have a bubble butt like you have?"

Again, utter confusion in her eyes as I continued. "Girl, you were born during the Kardashian phase of life! Have you seen the butts on those women? They have massive butts, and they are changing the perception of the world's idea of beauty!"

I continued, "You are actually blessed to have that bubble butt because there are thousands of women who spend money to try and get the exact shape of your butt!"

I went on to tell her how the ideal beauty when I was growing up was Kate Moss and 'heroin chic'. *Big* wasn't what a girl desired to be. Having triple D boobs, and a bigger frame, I was constantly uncomfortable in my own skin but was going to do my best to stop Sophia from thinking she was flawed and that her size was unacceptable because some bratty classmates decided to be mean.

I turned this moment around by creating another version of reality for her to perceive life as rather than the reality that I had lived in. I am not saying to use the Kardashians' lives as a

teachable moment (I mean, *geez*), but I do have to give them credit
for shifting the world's perception of beauty. Before they hit the
scene, society viewed the ideal shape of a woman to be young,
5'9, skinny as a rail, with a little waist and perky breasts. I must
commend retail companies now that showcase more realistic
models—this can help young girls see that most women are not
5'9 and 110 pounds. We are constantly bombarded by beauty in
the form of perfect faces and perfect bodies, our society makes
it hard to look at the person in the mirror and not feel less than.
We are surrounded by beauty but said beauty can be easily
manipulated by a filter, by a certain angle, creating an illusion of
perfection, where perfection doesn't exist.

Having daughters and knowing that they will be navigating a
minefield full of explosive devices (other people's and the world's
judgment of her body), I set forth that day to never talk about how
I felt about my body in a negative way, nor did I constantly praise
beauty as the end-all. I did not want their worth tied directly with
their external beauty. I wanted them to value their creativity,
kindness, compassion, internal drive and belief in who they are
inside.

Children look up to adults and when, let's say, Mom, is
constantly critical of her own appearance or is always pointing
out negative physical traits in others, it's hard not to create
opinions and thoughts based on what you are familiar with and
learn from. It is up to us, as adults, to celebrate the whole person,
praise their Soul rather than always focus on physical traits. Your
body changes all the time and when self-worth is tied up with
how one looks, it becomes a losing battle. We will all age, we will
all get wrinkles, we will all gain and lose weight throughout our
lives. Our Soul, though, remains constant and by being vigilant
about finding purpose and treating others with grace, life will have
more meaning. It's hard to do though, as we are constantly being
bombarded with images of perfection put on a pedestal.

With our phones glued to our hands, the icons of Insta and Facebook on the first screen, the ability to entertain ourselves at any moment, we tend to miss out on the present moments in life and start to create stories in our mind about how other people live (and get a case of FOMO, fear of missing out). This story or perception leads to unrealistic comparisons because you are not seeing a holistic view.

Yet, we seem like we can't ever get enough! Social media can feel like a never-ending adventure, where every swipe and scroll delivers a burst of excitement or much-needed reprieve. These are the feelings we assign to it. This burst comes from our brain releasing dopamine, making us feel good. It's like a mini reward for discovering interesting posts, getting likes, going viral (the END ALL BE ALL). We're drawn to keep scrolling because we're chasing those dopamine hits, seeking the next "like" or intriguing post. It's like a digital treasure hunt for our brains, and it's no wonder we sometimes find it hard to put our devices down. Our devices do not design or replace our desires; they actually work as a distraction tool to keep us from truly seeking what it is we desire in our lives.

The way to begin to uncover who you are and what you desire is to stop the negative thoughts about yourself and begin realizing that no one sees one body part. You are composed of so many parts and people see ALL of you, so you need to begin to see ALL of you.

Change your thoughts about yourself, change your reality. Be grateful for the parts you don't like because they still serve you and make you unique! If you don't like the size of your thighs, write down a daily affirmation that you are grateful for your big thighs because they are strong and can carry you for miles and miles. This is how you break the cycle. This is hard to do when the focus on that specific body part is hard to love, but every part of you, good, bad, ugly, scarred, and imperfect, creates the body you have been given. Train your brain to appreciate, not criticize. The only person you are hurting by criticizing yourself is you.

# Chapter 15

# VIP DIETER



"The discipline of desire is the background of character."

—*John Locke*

Some of the headlines from the last thirty years pushed out from the diet and fitness industry would read: "Calories In/Calories Out is your way to slim." "Get going on the Low-Fat Diet/Zone Diet/Weight Watchers/Keto Diet/Paleo Diet/Carnivores Diet to drop 50 pounds!" "Keep your heart rate in zone 2 for fat burning." "Run for over 45 minutes/HIIT training/Spinning/Cross fit!" Each of these marketing messages not only made people buy but also, cemented the idea that one-size-fits-all wellness works for everyone the same. Nope. False hope once again.

In 1989, to my absolute glee, Ashley Richardson, considered "full figured", made it on the front page of the SI edition. She looked like me and you know what "me" I was referring to? A woman with long, blond hair, bigger thighs, thicker waist, big boobs, a tiny bit of a belly (not concave like the *Vogue* models) and broad shoulders. She looked like an Amazon woman and that made me feel pretty good, temporarily. This was way before Ashley Graham graced the cover and Target had full size images of normal looking girls in bathing suits on display. This was also during the time Kate Moss and 'heroin chic' was the staple of beauty so I didn't have many women to look up to that had a similar look to myself. Ashley proceeded to grace the cover of the magazine six more times, so to me, that gave me hope that what women strive to be (size 2, skinny, tall), wasn't what the opposite sex thought was sexy and perfect.

This made me feel a tiny bit better about my big frame but certainly didn't make a dent in my negative self-talk or body dysmorphia. I still looked in the mirror with a hand on my stomach trying to push it in constantly, weighing myself twice a day and obsessing over the number of the scale. I was what someone would call a "chronic dieter", as I would research and keep up with the latest diet trends like they were celebrities on the cover of *People* magazine.

Jane Fonda put exercise on the map, but Weight Watchers, Jenny Craig, and The Zone Diet put yoyo dieting right in front our eyes with Jennifer Aniston praising it as her miracle solution. And why not? Using illusion, these companies would convince individuals to spend thousands on boxed food, supplements, meetings and shakes in the hopes of becoming a size 2. To put it bluntly, big industries and corporations are driven by one force: making a profit so in order to keep earning a profit, they need to just repackage the old diets and bingo!

It's not necessarily evil, but it's crucial to recognize that everything bombarding you daily aims to provoke action. Work for a company, buy products, attend services, scroll through social media—every move you make contributes to the flow of money. Money is the fuel that powers the engine of our world. Capitalism, in many ways, has transformed lives globally for the better, but here's some insight: you have a say in whether their influence steers your actions so taking personal responsibility and guarding yourself against external influence are pivotal in maintaining control over your choices and your life.

When I became certified in nutrition seventeen years ago, my understanding of the diet industry was intimate, having been a paying member since the age of 5 so this topic, along with exercise, is part of who I am. However, the depth of knowledge surrounding our food industry, the government's role, and the lobbyists' substantial influence on governmental laws and guidelines, were entirely foreign to me. Initially, my focus was solely on understanding how food interacts with my body to detach emotionally from it and perceive it more as fuel rather than tied to an emotion.

I vividly recall the impact of the "low fat" diet craze—an era where not only the diet and food industries, but the government too, were endorsing this trend. However, the no-fat diet only caused me weight gain, mental struggle, and a distorted self-image. If I could turn back time, I would urge young Amy to disregard the diet industry and governmental guidelines, encouraging her to turn inward, understand her own nutritional needs and nourishing her body with real food. My past experiences, which led to my binge eating disorder, shaped me and guided me to where I stand today. My aspiration is to shed light on our food system, the diet industry, the government's food pyramid, and other related subjects to awaken you to the constant marketing bombardment. Awareness is the first step toward reclaiming control.

If you talk about the diet industry, you must gain insight into the younger sister, so meet the fitness industry! The fitness industry has been a rollercoaster ride of trends, promises, and marketing campaigns, often pitching the latest exercise fad as the ultimate solution to achieving fitness goals. From the 1970s onward, it's been a whirlwind.

Mentioning Jane Fonda again, with her leotard, slim belt, sweatband and leg warmers on the floor doing leg lifts, think about how fucking incredible the marketing campaign was back then and how that celebrity inspired millions to start sweating! Talk about a powerful message. The rise of home workout videos made sweating to the beat a cultural phenomenon with housewives working out in their living rooms while little Johnny sat in the playpen. It seemed like the perfect formula—follow the moves, keep up the pace, and voilà, fitness magic and you will look just like Jane Fonda! But here's the catch: While aerobics, including running, spinning, Zumba and Step, have benefits, again, not a one-size-fits-all solution.

Spinning classes and running groups joined the scene to shoot up the endorphins and create comradery for members to feel a part of a group. Running and spinning do torch calories, but again, calories in/calories out is a myth as a one-size-fits-all solution. DNA, age, glucose levels, hormones, lifestyle and effort play a significant role here. That did not prevent the explosion of boutique studios, like CrossFit, SoulCycle and big gyms like Life Time, which took on a cult-like following. The promise of functional movements, high intensity, and camaraderie drew in enthusiasts.

Next came boutique barre, Pilates and yoga places which again, created a community effect yet promised something that it could not deliver. Individuals got hooked on the familiar routine and environment, going 4/5/6/7 times a week yet, did not typically witness any change in their body composition.

It always boggled my mind when someone would talk to me about how they wanted to lose 20 pounds and had been doing spin classes at a high intensity almost every day, and were frustrated that their body didn't respond. I would be too! All that sweat and time spent, at least you could get the body you desire, right?

Enter places like Orange Theory, Blast900 and F45, which combine functional training and high-intensity interval training (HIIT) on regular or curved treadmills. The allure of group sessions and varied workouts where you go back and forth between cardio and strength training gained traction. Yet again, the "one-size-fits-all" assumption hits a roadblock—what works wonders for one might not for another.

Because women especially are not taught how to strength train (today is different for female athletes in high school and college so I am talking about those of us who are past college age), the idea of strength training wasn't ingrained in our minds at an early age, like our male friends. Who could forget Arnold or the buff David Hasselhoff? Boys with raging testosterone during puberty, have the desire to get big and strong as biologically, their brains are wired for battle and protection, and they work out intensely after school and during sports. Muscles equal strength equals dominance. Let's face it: In high school, many of us women were too busy starving ourselves to be small and impress boys. We are wired to nurture and thus, strength training is not really promoted as a way of getting in touch with your feminine side.

Trust me when I say I did not always recognize strength training as a critical component to my well-being. Having always "worked out", meaning cardio, I never thought weights were necessary because I was already bigger boned, until Roman Fortin got a hold of me. Plus, magazines back then featured models who were skin and bones so who thought that muscles could be sexy? You didn't see many lean, muscular women walking around as you do today.

We are aging every second of every day and I cannot stress to you enough the importance of building and maintaining lean muscle mass to ensure vitality and well-being. Working my fast twitch muscles became a game changer, as I detailed in Chapter 4, and changed my body composition faster and better than any other workout program out there. My goal is to be eighty and still lifting weights, and it will happen!

Before I began my journey of uncovering big agendas, I was always confused as to why I was constantly dieting yet kept gaining weight. I mean, if I am not eating fat, how can I look fatter in the mirror? I was young and impressionable and glommed on whatever new diet or food fad there was to try because I wanted hope. I was desperate to change my body and like always buying lottery tickets, I thought, *maybe this next one is the winner!*

Going on a diet, then off a diet, then repeat again is called yoyo dieting, which impacts your body and creates chaos in your mind, as deprivation and restriction become the outline for which you must follow, along with weighing your food, counting macros, and other behavior patterns you must adhere to in order to be successful. As I plunged deeper into my study of how the diet and fitness industry pushes products, I couldn't help but begin examining our food system in a different light. Little did I know how deep the rabbit hole I would go to understand the entwined relationship between the government and food corporations, and the pivotal role of marketing in shaping societal behavior.

As a population, we look to the government for guidance on areas including education, laws, taxes and this massive entity also wants to guide us on how we eat. Think about this for a moment: we are relying on a massive conglomerate that takes money from industries and tells the public what is best. Again, shame on all of us for giving away the power we each must make choices based on our bodies. Back in the 1980s, the government's food guide pyramid had four levels. The bottom level included bread, cereal, rice, and pasta, with a recommended 6 to 11 servings per day. The second level was split between a vegetable group (3 to 5 servings per day) and a fruit group (2 to 4 servings per day).

Cereal/breads/grains were used as the foundation of our daily diets. *What?* No wonder myself and millions of Americans steadily gained weight after this pyramid was put into place. Follow the money. If you study the food pyramid, we should be eating mostly simple carbs, followed by vegetables (carbs), fruit (carbs), with a little protein, and very little fat. Why not trust the government? After all, they know how my body works, right? Due to public pressure and the rise of obesity and sugar consumption, in 2011, the government could no longer deny that their recommendation of grains and cereals was leading to health problems, and finally tweaked the recommendation. For almost twenty years, we were told how great simple carbohydrates were and that fat was the enemy. The results were disastrous on an individual level yet, many industries benefited by the rise in inflammation and obesity, which again, brings to light the power of money over your wellness.

The new recommendation became a plate with veggies as the bigger portion, and protein was put back into a better slice of the pie. But still, grains were as big as vegetables, which means that along with fruit (carbohydrates), vegetables (carbohydrates), and grains (carbohydrates), your recommended daily food intake is about 60-80% carbohydrates. Notice there is no part of the plate that has fats on it? So, if you were someone who has not researched food, you would probably assume that fat is still the enemy. Dairy, which is a carbohydrate and a fat (unless it is skim), is off to the side tucked away. Who makes money on this recommendation? Food manufactures are still cashing in, and if you examine our medical system, Big Pharma and insurance companies are eating up a huge chunk of money because of the rapid rise in obesity, heart disease, diabetes and other ailments. Taking initiative for our own wellness requires thoughts and actions. Our blind spots can be caused by the desire to alleviate pain.

# Chapter 16

# AGE OF ENLIGHTENMENT

"Within all of us is a divine capacity to manifest and attract all that we need and desire."

—*Wayne Dyer*

We hate being uncomfortable both physically and emotionally, right? We want to eliminate pain so we can go about our day, and it's a common desire to alleviate pain promptly so that we can continue the daily grind uninterrupted, isn't it? Let's delve into pain because whether we recognize it or not, any form of pain affects our entire being and the synergy of mind, body and Soul is impacted if we let pain linger. Consider the impact of pain, be it physical from an injury or emotional from lingering childhood experiences or trauma, has on your well-being. When you are nursing a knee injury, that pain affects every part of you and can mess with your mood, your outlook and your activity level. The same is true when we are in pain from loss of a loved one, heartbreak from a failed relationship or cannot seem to shake the emotions and feelings of unaddressed childhood trauma, hiding in your subconscious mind.

God never promised a smooth and easy life and as much as parents want to bubble-wrap their kids, being alive means we will endure and get through many types of pain in our lives. Try to think about pain in a different way so rather than trying immediately to eliminate pain, think about pain as your body's signal to your brain that something is imbalanced within and pay closer attention. Our reaction is to pop a pill to make pain go away. Mask the pain and thus, move on to more enjoyable tasks.

Yet the ailment might remain, masked and silenced for a moment. If we don't try and uncover why the pain was there in the first place, the imbalance will continue. Our body, mind and Soul crave homeostasis, which is the most optimal and balanced way of living. Pain is a signal that something needs attention within, whether that is a physical pain, like knee pain, or a physical pain in your heart from heartbreak. Our emotions are stored in our subconscious mind and can manifest within our body in different ways. That is why your heart can physically hurt when you break up with someone, or your stomach is in knots from anxiety over an upcoming deadline. The emotion manifests itself within the body part and if not recognized, can wreak havoc on all parts of you.

When we don't look into our pain, we prolong our healing and prevent homeostasis within.

I used to be this way. Any hint of ailment, issue or pain prompted me to schedule a doctor appointment at the sign of any discomfort. Ten years ago, I learned the valuable lesson of "pausing" before acting regardless of who is giving you the advice or treatment.

Anyone love broccoli? Raise your hand. Anyone? No? Well, you are looking at a girl who LOVES broccoli. It's one of my top five foods and I consume it almost every day. I know I am not the norm, but something in my body and mind craves broccoli almost as much as I crave ice cream. This craving is part body, part mind because remember, I was told not to fill up my plate and was constantly told to diet and broccoli is a big vegetable that takes up a lot of space on a plate, which is why I love seeing it.

Without changing my broccoli habit, I started to experience severe stomach pains at night. Not only gas, but pain and bloating to the point where I looked six months pregnant. This went on for about a month and it became alarming because I hadn't changed anything about what I was eating so I finally saw a gastro doctor. As the good doctor asked me about my symptoms, I told him all about my internal gas pain, severe stomach bloat and how uncomfortable I was every night. He told me he had to rule out specific diagnosis, and the way he would do it was to order a biopsy of my stomach lining, my small colon, large colon, and submit a stool sample. *Holy shit* was my first thought, as I continued to listen to him describe the procedure I would endure, including sedating me, sticking a tube down my throat, cutting a tiny piece of my colon, as well as my stomach lining, and more. I was expecting to be prescribed some medication and sent on my way.

As I left the office, I was totally freaked out because that seemed like an extreme protocol to rule out some of the digestive disorders out there. Later that night, when Steven got home, he asked what the doctor said about my pain. I told him the list of things that the good doctor had told me he had to "rule out" first and then by process of elimination, would make his best educated guess about how to fix the problem. Here is something everyone needs to read, absorb and never forget: Doctors *practice* medicine. They really do not know how an individual will react to a procedure, protocol or drug because each human body is unique.

Steven then asked a question that hit me like a ton of bricks. "Did he ask you what you eat?" I replied no, he never had me describe my diet or anything about food. Now, I understand doctors study for seven years learning about the human body, how it works, what diseases are prevalent, and keep up with the vast amount of data and information. Kind of like "walking encyclopedias". So naturally, a doctor who specializes in gastrointestinal disorders would also know that food impacts this system.

I hate to point this out but most of the time, we blindly give away our power to doctors who are literally *practicing* medicine on us using pharmaceutical drugs to help mask pain. We go to a doctor with an ailment and typically, leave the office with one or more drugs to solve the ailment. We don't ask questions much, because we tend to believe (this is what most are taught to believe) that an individual who went to school to study medicine knows more about our bodies than we do. We assume that the doctor has done extensive research about the medication, what the side effects are, and then weighs it against what they know about us from the couple minutes spent with us.

That doctor has roughly seven minutes to walk in, shake my hand, create the warm and fuzzies, ask target questions about my symptoms, order the nurse to fill the script, and walks out. On average, he sees fifty patients each day. Doctors rely on Big Pharma to create the drugs and then they experiment with the drug to determine if it fixes the pain or aliment. Sometimes you notice a big difference when you take the meds, and sometimes you don't notice anything is different. Now, understand, I am a huge fan of the medical community and believe we live in the greatest country because our healthcare system is still private, but that doesn't mean doctors should be given complete authority over our bodies when it comes to healing and pain.

Food is medicine and can act like a drug when ingested, impacting every cell in the body. Humans have been using plants and animal byproducts to cure all sorts of diseases and pain for millions of years, so the lack of nutritional knowledge taught in medical school is staggering and not easy to comprehend. A medical student spends 4 years plus another 3 years of residency, working and studying between 40 and 80 hours, so we are looking at over 20,000 hours at least before they can be called "doctor". Of the over 20,000 hours, about 25 hours or .00125% of their time is spent understanding how food interacts with the body? Food for thought that should give you pause!

If medical school placed more emphasis on nutrition and the connection between food, pain, feelings and emotions, I believe the broccoli doctor would have immediately asked me to describe my typical day of nutrition to rule out food sensitivity. He could have asked if I was stressed or anxious. Maybe rather than writing up the script to put me under the knife, he would have said the following: "I know you have an extreme love affair with broccoli. This is a new ailment that suddenly appeared last month so why don't we rule out broccoli as the cause of the extreme stomach bloating to determine if the response was from a change in your gut? As the saying goes, "Listen to your body," which might have been a better option for me than going under the knife.

Rather than schedule the procedure, I conducted my own "trial", and stopped eating broccoli for three weeks, took a probiotic supplement to help establish homeostasis within my stomach lining and journaled how I felt each night. My body healed from the broccoli reprieve and the probiotics I found over the counter! I was having a reaction to broccoli for some reason but giving my stomach and gut three weeks with no green trees, I cured myself of the ailment and began my habit of eating broccoli with dinner every night after, with no pain, might I add.

Sadly, to him, not me, the doctor was not going to make any money telling me to lay off the broccoli for a couple weeks, journal, and report the findings back to him. Again, so appreciative of doctors, but they are in the business to take pain away (pharma) and/or cut into you and are not practicing medicine to heal you. I do not blame the good doctor though because I am responsible for my body and what I put into my body. I can be told by countless doctors, experts, researchers, marketing companies, what I should be ingesting, but I get to make the final decision because it is my body. And, might I add, the only body I have ever been given and will ever have. I did not have to be sedated, cut into, or biopsied to heal myself. Talk about ROI—I alone prevented further pain, hassle and time, while saving money on a hellacious procedure. I cured myself because I didn't settle for the opinion of another. I have never forgotten that valuable lesson.

What was eye opening during my researching phase was that I began to see alternative treatments or remedies that had once been vilified and disgraced, including the vilified marijuana plant. I don't know about you, but I was raised during the "just say no to drugs" slogan from Nancy Reagan, with images of potheads wandering the streets aimlessly, as the picture was painted that drugs such as marijuana, mushrooms, LSD and Ketamine were dangerous and deadly. I never wanted to be a pothead and had never experimented with any drugs (besides alcohol) as a teenager because the fear of God was instilled in me at such a young, impressionable age. *Try it once, and you can never go back.* Scary message. Not as scary as what happened to thousands who became hooked on Oxycontin, but I digress.  Opioids are the deadliest drug type killing more than three times as many people as cocaine. OD deaths rank just below diabetes in terms of highest death count, yet were prescribed nonstop by doctors everywhere, while TCH and mushrooms remained locked up and hidden away.

As my understanding and insight about drugs, in general grew, my opinion changed as I realized that, like our food manufactures in bed with our government, so was the pharmaceutical industry. Following the money trail can be very eye opening and as some states began to legalize marijuana, COVID-19 entered our lives with Big Pharma sprinting behind to capitalize on our fears.

Four years ago, I was amid an existential crisis of life and felt I was a hamster on a wheel running so hard, that I not only lost who I was, but also, how I reacted to the world. My emotions were high, my daily life consisted of waking up at 6:45 a.m., getting the kids dressed, fed and driven to school, turning around and driving to the gym to teach a fitness class or two, before showering, dressing and jumping in the car to do my corporate job. Then running at a high pace during the workday, I would drive home, put my "Mom!" hat on, and continue to run until I got them to bed, to which I then had to put in my notes and data in (think TPS reports) from my time in the field that day. I was running from morning until night, with my only reprieve when I gave myself forty-five minutes to read in bed before shutting the light off. I lived at a pace that was unsustainable long term, and my energy level was drained from every orifice.

Because of my belief system I carried with me throughout life, I felt I had to soldier on and keep working harder and better. Consequently, I was quick to anger, screaming when frustrated, and the whole family began tiptoeing around me. Steven suggested I go the doctor because I was so up and down. I was once prescribed an antidepressant, Prozac, before my wedding yet never took it, remember? With my life in internal chaos, and with the approval of Steven, I looked at Prozac as something I could try in order to continue on the treadmill of daily life. Easy, quick, and effortless to take.

I didn't ever have time, so this pill would help me mask my thoughts and feelings about where I was in life, how unfulfilled I felt and where the deep-seated resentment and frustration was coming from. Pop the pill to put a smile on! I needed to understand where the agitation was coming from, rather than minimize it, but at this point, I wasn't aware of anything woo-woo or heady and had no thought about understanding my feelings. I needed to stuff them back down into my subconscious mind because they were inconvenient and annoying. If I was unwilling to stop and become present to my feelings, how could I define and drive my desired life?

Fast forward to the year I call "the dark time" when a friend introduced me to CBD gummies as a way of calming my anxiety and stress. I was intrigued because I was not a drinker, due to incredibly horrific hangovers which eliminated any desire to have more than one drink at a social function. Further, neither Steven nor I had ever tried illegal drugs so I didn't pay attention to CBD or TCH because again, they were illegal until they weren't and didn't play a part in my world. The vision of a stoned Brad Pitt in the movie "True Romance" would be top of mind if the word *marijuana* was mentioned, which was actually a nice visual but kept marijuana at bay.

We, as energy beings, crave synergy of mind, body and Soul. When something in the body is signaling pain, the mind is affected, outlook on life gets impacted and energy drops so I dove into the data and research with an open and inquisitive mind because after reading about why the government shut down the studies on psychedelic drugs during the Nixon era and beyond, it was hard not to see who was making money by creating artificial versions of drugs found in the wild. It's important to note that, like pharmaceutical drugs, these products have individual effects and interactions on you, based on dosage, personal tolerance, and other factors unique to you and are not a one-size-fits-all miracle drug.

What I most appreciate about CBD is that like Omega-3 fatty acids, it has anti-inflammatory properties that can help reduce inflammation in the body, which is often associated with pain. Like Advil or other drugs created in a lab to reduce inflammation, CBD interacts with both CB1 and CB2 receptors in the ECS and can influence pain signaling pathways and might also help with neuropathic pain by signaling and, potentially reducing the sensations of burning, shooting, or tingling pain. Most illnesses are a result of inflammation, heart disease, diabetes, cancer and arthritis are just a sampling, so if you ingest anti-inflammatory agents like Omega-3 or CBD, that helps counteract the internal inflammation.

I am not telling you this, so you run out and buy, just to be open minded about alternative avenues that go against the conventional beliefs we are fed. These beliefs might not be in our best interest and typically benefit a big industry. It's your body so you need to take time to research and find solutions on your own because again, you know your body best. Remember, the answers you seek for your trajectory are within. In conjunction, there are many tools for healing wounds, both physically and emotionally, to help you find yourself again and reigniting desire you have buried within yourself. Be sure that whatever you decide to ingest, do it with thoughtfulness, whether it be a pill, a gummy, an opinion or suggestion. It is always your choice.

# Chapter 17

# MY DESIRE EMPIRE



I always dreamed about waking up and spending twenty minutes writing in a journal, before I start going about my day. I knew it was an outstanding habit to have, and people that journaled seemed to have their shit together. They allowed themselves time, without picking up their phone, without rushing to get the kids up, in order to  put their thoughts and feelings down onto paper, from visualized thoughts into physical words. It sounded like such a calm and peaceful habit to implement into a daily practice. As a "quick start", I didn't take the time to analyze what journaling would give back to me, in exchange for the twenty minutes I was giving to it. I simply liked the calming image in my mind of writing in my leather-bound journal, as the sun rose, with a mug of coffee on the table next to me. I had attempted to journal before, when I was pregnant with each of my children, but as life got busier and more hectic, I spent less energy on recording my thoughts and feelings as they each grew. Cason's baby journal was completed, and I ended up buying a second one to continue writing in. Sophia's was just about finished, Colt about halfway through and poor Brookie Cookie, I think I only have around fifty pages written for her. Writing that makes me want to pick up the label "bad mom" but I will stop myself. I figure I remember more about her childhood because I am older so that's how I justify it in my mind.

Here's the thing, I told myself I hated to write, so the baby journals were a labor of love, yet I had the opinion in my mind that it was a chore, like folding laundry. Essential when complete, but not a lot of fun while you are sitting there trying to make a perfect square.

During my divorce, I finally realized that I had been carrying around a label for years that did not actually align with who I was. I didn't believe I was a good writer or any kind of writer because back in eighth grade, one of my English teachers said to me that I had no talent for writing. This teacher, let's call him Mr. Grey, was sarcastic and kind of a dick and had the nerve to tell me I was a bad writer. So, what did thirteen-year-old Amy do? The same thing she did when Dr. X made a judgment about her eight years prior. Amy believed it and ran with it. She went through life using his label like a badge of honor, always making sure people around her knew she was a "bad writer". She suppressed her talent and never thought to discard that label.

During my dark time, I began journaling as a way of coping with loneliness and self-imposed isolation. I finally decided I didn't give a fuck that Mr. Grey had that opinion or which I carried around with me because I had so much to say to the world as I began to find my true voice again, and hot damn, I am going to write whatever comes to mind and not give a fuck about comma placement. I It took me over thirty years to say "fuck it" to that label I had carried. Here I am, readers!

Never in my wildest dreams did I think I could write a book, let alone two. Once I dropped the label that contrasted who I am, I started to crave journaling as an outlet, giving me freedom to express myself any way I wanted. I journaled so much that I saw what I had inside me that needed to be expressed and shared with others. Movement on the page, like ballet. Letters progressing into words and sentences, the choreography of thought into story. Like dancing was my creative outlet for my body, writing became a creative outlet for my mind and Soul. What freedom!

From my past, I carried with me labels preventing me from exploring the world and living a life I designed. Writing a book was never on my radar, like, not even a speck, because I thought I could not write. Journaling broke through this thought pattern and as the words effortlessly found the page, I went from thinking writing was a chore, to finding writing cathartic and healing.

A business coach actually gave me the courage to write my story, and right after reading an excerpt, said, "You know, Amy, you have a great story and I like your writing style, you should write a book!" *Boom.* Released from the self-imposed shackles, I started to write and couldn't stop. I wrote for six straight weeks, from 7:00 a.m. to 3:00 p.m. on a mission. I felt compelled to tell my story, so that I could inspire someone else struggling with body dysmorphia and self-limiting beliefs.

As I began to understand the power of the mind, the words, *visualization* and *manifestation* found their way to me. Thinking they were silly in the past, during my writing phase, I started to understand these powerful concepts and witnessing events in my own life that told me there was more out there for me to learn about the world, universe and God.

My first experience with understanding manifestation and visualization happened through a set of synchronistic events. Right before I began writing *Big Desire* and my follow-up, *The Desire Method*, I was still journaling as a way of coping with the change and void left in me when I didn't have my children around.

I happen to be on a Zoom call with a client and one of our consultants, Krishna, who hailed from Long Island. Having only spoken via phone a couple times, I liked Krishna, but did not really know him well. So, after the client jumped off the Zoom session, something in me prevented me from dropping off as well. I can't recall what happened but for some reason, Krishna and I stayed on the phone, and I confessed to him how lost I felt in life. I had wanted to get divorced but had not anticipated the sheer loneliness and struggle of changing my life so drastically. He told me to start meditating and to look into the Silva Method. I promised I would, wrote it down, and found it interesting that I opened up to him so easily. I wasn't used to being vulnerable, remember?

Three weeks later, I received a text from Krishna, telling me he thought of me and that I should read the book, *The Power of Intention*, by Wayne Dyer. I thanked him, but it would be another three weeks before I thought to take his advice.

I happened to be driving Sophia to Nashville for a one-day volleyball tournament, so the total drive time was eight hours. A multitasker at heart, knowing she would sleep the whole way (the girl is a sleeper!), I would listen to the Audible version in the car. As the words were read to me, a lightbulb went off in my mind and suddenly the world changed colors on me. The concept of living in the moment, with intention and visualizing what you desire in life, was the foundation of the book and what I was hearing was so vastly different from cookie cutter, it blew my mind.

I was furiously making voice notes on my phone and one word stuck out to me, with its beauty and its meaning: *synchronicity*. Synchronicity is when two or more events happen at the same time in a way that feels meaningful, even though they don't have a direct cause-and-effect relationship. Imagine thinking about an old friend you haven't seen in years, and then bumping into them later that day. It feels like more than just a coincidence, right? That's synchronicity! Carl Jung, a famous psychologist coined the term and called it "meaningful coincidences" that connect our thoughts to the outside world.

In this vein, as I finished Dyer's book, I texted Krishna to thank him for the recommendation. "This book is life changing for me," I wrote. He immediately texted back with a picture of that very same book, where he had at that moment been underlying a passage for which to send to me.  The passage in the book described how most spend their lives driving their own boat but are too busy looking back at the wake (past) to realize the sheer possibilities life holds for you, if only you looked in front of you (present and future). The vast ocean of possibilities—how exhilarating!  The concept reinforced the very moment I finished the book on Saturday afternoon on my way home from Nashville, with Krishna sitting in his house in Long Island, underlining a passage to send to me in that same book. As if a double whammy, he texted "synchronicity", which was the very last word I had captured on my Notes app.  Talk about the hair on your arms standing up, I tell you this because events started happening to me that guided me on this journey to where I am now and because I began meditating daily, quieting my mind to pray, visualizing what exactly I desire in life (down to what I am wearing and doing and being), and manifesting my dreams became a very powerful and very real vehicle for which this would happen.

I knew my story could help people and so I found my purpose and my passion from the darkness I was living.

The word, *manifestation*, stirs both positive and negative emotions, depending on the individual and their beliefs. When someone would say to me "I manifested *XYZ*," I thought they had lost their mind. My judgment, based on fear, was that this person was too free-spirited, worshipped Mother Earth and must have a screw loose and therefore, was a bit on the wild and dangerous side. Now? I am a true believer in the power of manifesting what you want in your life because guess what, we already create our realities. In recognizing the power to guide our realities through manifesting is where it really gets interesting.

Manifestation isn't some mystical hocus-pocus. It's about aligning your thoughts, beliefs, and actions with what you want through mindful visualization. Think of it as placing an order in a restaurant. You're not just wishing for food; you're declaring which meal you want to eat specifically and then believing when it is ready,  the waiter will bring it out to you because it is yours.

To manifest what you desire, you need to get crystal clear on what you want. Vague wishes won't cut it. Be specific. See it, feel it, taste it in your mind. Then, believe it's possible. Not just surface-level belief, but deep-in-your-bones certainty. Your subconscious needs to be on board.

Next, act as if. If you want to be a successful entrepreneur, start thinking and behaving like one now. Dress the part. Make decisions as if you're already there. Your actions send powerful signals to your brain and the world around you.

Here's the kicker: you can't just sit on your couch and expect miracles. Manifestation requires action. It's about creating opportunities, being open to possibilities, and having the guts to say yes when they show up. It's putting in the work while maintaining unwavering faith that what you want is on its way to you.

Remember, manifesting isn't about controlling every detail. It's about setting the intention, doing the work, and then letting go. Trust the process. The universe and God might have an even better plan than you imagined.

Ever wondered why certain people become famous while others don't? Start googling Jim Carey, Oprah, Jennifer Anniston, and many other celebrities and you will hear them talk about manifesting their careers. It's not that they were more talented, better looking or luckier than others. It was that they believed they will be famous, so all their thoughts aligned with that belief and their behaviors/habits/actions matched this belief. That is the power of manifesting.

If you know now you can control your thoughts and you know what direction you want your life to go in, visualization, journaling and reprogramming your subconscious mind is all part of manifesting what you desire. Be specific in your vision, including how you feel, touch, taste, smell and see. Be as imaginative as possible because like I said earlier, your subconscious mind is a computer program, and you hold all the power in what goes into that program. It's time to rewrite your program and remove what is holding you back. Focus on passion and purpose instead of meaningless outputs and busy work.

Whether you are aware or not, you already manifest things into your life through your thoughts, beliefs and actions. Take this example – I hear Taylor Swift is coming to my city and my thoughts go like this: OMG I can't wait! The tickets are going to be so expensive, but I can make it work! As my thoughts are forming, my mind is creating a visual picture of the future experience, with the lights, atmosphere, songs, Taylor in her sequin outfit, me singing along and dancing in the isles! My body starts to respond to the vision by increasing my heart rate, producing happy feelings of joy and anticipation, which leads me to smile big and start singing a line from Anti Hero. At that moment, I manifested what my life was going to look like, on that date in the future and my body created an emotional attachment to the event.

If you are manifesting already, you just need to harness the power by making sure your thoughts align with what you want to create in your life. These thoughts are not just passive mental processes; they trigger a cascade of emotions within us, from joy and anticipation to excitement. Although the event itself hasn't transpired, our bodies respond as if it were real, creating emotional responses tied to those thoughts. This is what big manifestation is all about. It's a mental rehearsal of the life you desire so all of you is in alignment for when it happens.

In the grand scheme of intentional living, visualizing your dreams so they manifest into your reality, sparks the creative process, igniting the imagination and setting the stage. Manifestation breathes life into your visions, transforming them from thoughts into tangible realities. The easiest way to create your dream is by visualizing, journaling and repetition. The more you think about your life in a way you have created in your mind, the more it gets stored in your subconscious as a program and during your waking hours, you will be open to see the synchronicities and experiences that happen as your manifestation begins to take shape.

The act of simply using the power of my mind to create the life I desire is now how I operate each day. I no longer watch the news, listen to politics, read about celebrities or allow my TV to be broadcasting murder mysteries or crime shows. I protect my subconscious mind fiercely because knowing I have the power to create the life I desire, means protecting what goes into my subconscious thoughts and beliefs. I took my power back from society, and I am holding it near and dear to my heart.

My life now? I write. I dance. I dream. I create. I inspire. I desire. And I manifest.

We lose the connection to who we are sometimes, when society gets a hold of us. But we can find ourselves again. That is what God wants for us all—to find our authentic selves.

# Chapter 18

# BIG LITTLE STAR



"Life ought to be a struggle of desire toward adventures whose nobility will fertilize the soul."

—*Rebecca West*

I won't sugarcoat it—change is brutal. Our central nervous system is designed to keep us safe, defaulting to autopilot in familiar situations. But when faced with change? Holy crap, look out. Our minds and bodies start losing their shit, chaos ensuing as internal programs battle for dominance.

A quote echoes in my mind: "People will always choose a familiar, comfortable hell over an unfamiliar heaven." Think about that friend constantly complaining about her boyfriend, job, body, or mother. Or perhaps it's you? The culprit is familiarity, seasoned with societal norms and opinions, keeping us stagnant.

Here's the truth—change is hard, but you know what's harder? Regret. That gut-wrenching feeling on your deathbed when you realize your life's worries and pursuits had nothing to do with your Soul's desires but everything to do with society's dictates. You'll reflect and understand that only relationships truly matter, and the longest relationship you'll ever have is with...yourself. You can run, hide, mask, and wallow, but you can never escape yourself.

So why not stop running? Turn inward and truly listen to the little person inside you—she's closer to your authentic self than anyone else. She's desperate for your attention, shouting and waving her arms frantically. She loves you unconditionally and wants you to rediscover her, to lead the life she knows you're capable of living. She's begging you to release the heavy rocks you've collected on life's path—they were never yours to carry.

I wish someone had grabbed my broad, strong shoulders when I was an innocent, little girl, telling me to stay true to who I was. Don't change for the world. Don't believe everything you're told because your talent and voice needs to be seen and heard. Would that have made a difference? I am not sure, but the optimist in me thinks so.

I was born into a precut, cookie-cutter life template designed to keep me safe, comfortable, and conforming. The goal? Minimize hurt, struggle, and pain. The reality? It amplifies life's struggles, compounds pain, and breeds emotional turmoil I was ill-equipped to handle.

I am not any different than you. That inner voice you have gets silenced, even though she knows you better than anyone and longs for reunion. She's witnessed your journey through dark valleys as the world hurled stones and darts. She's waited patiently, through rock bottoms, for you to face her again.

We lose ourselves in life, fed beliefs from an early age, absorbing others' opinions and judgments, creating personas that don't reflect our true selves. We lose the person God created— that little spark, the essence of who we are, the Soul that knows our deepest desires, hopes, and dreams. Our Souls get beaten, silenced, shamed, guilted, told to fall in line and obey.

All those material things we're told matter, all the ways we're supposed to conform to belong—do they fulfill us at our core? You know you can't take money, cars, bags, or reputation with you when you're gone. It's all temporary. What endures is the love within your heart because unconditional love drives life. Everyone strives to give and receive love. Your relationship with yourself, your family, and others in this world—these are life's purpose.

Yet we settle for less, accepting society's opinion as absolute truth rather than living authentically for our purpose.

My best friend, Megan, posed a poignant question after reading my  manuscript: "Amy, if you could go back in time, kneel down and look directly into little Amy's big, green eyes, full of hope and wonder for a sparkly, glittering future, what would you tell her? What would you say to shield her from the internal pain she went through?"

As my eyes welled up with tears, the question hit me hard. After a long pause, I realized what I would say to Little Star—the name I now use when I speak to her, which I do often to maintain our connection and assure her of my protection. I would tell her: "Little Star, don't let society snuff out that inner spark within you. Your desire to be big and bold and your most authentic self needs to shine brightly. Don't hide away the parts of you that you deem imperfect, because God made every part of you, and He doesn't make mistakes. He never promised an easy life, but He did promise unconditional love. Know that you are never alone. God is always in you, with you, and beside you."

Standing up, I would run my hand over my flat stomach, the Mannino pooch no longer evident, just quiet memories of the place where my four children grew. I would add this final truth: "Even though there was such internal strife and heartbreak, I wouldn't change a thing. Every experience and every lesson learned brought me back to you, Little Star."